how to
click

Also by Trevor Silvester:

Lovebirds

how to click

The art of dating with confidence

TREVOR SILVESTER

CORONET

First published in Great Britain in 2015 by Coronet
An imprint of Hodder & Stoughton
An Hachette UK company

First published in paperback in 2016

1

A CIP catalogue record for this title is available from the British Library

Paperback ISBN: 978 1 444 74095 0
Ebook ISBN: 978 1 444 74094 3

Typeset in Plantin Light by Palimpsest Book Production Ltd,
Falkirk, Stirlingshire

Printed and bound by Clays Ltd, St Ives plc

Hodder & Stoughton policy is to use papers that are natural, renewable and
recyclable products and made from wood grown in sustainable forests. The
logging and manufacturing processes are expected to conform to the
environmental regulations of the country of origin.

Hodder & Stoughton Ltd
Carmelite House
50 Victoria Embankment
London EC4Y 0DZ

www.hodder.co.uk

Contents

Introduction vii

CHAPTER ONE: How to be your best dating self . . . 1

CHAPTER TWO: How to get in the dating zone. . . .31

CHAPTER THREE: Meeting your date 41

CHAPTER FOUR: How to get to know your date,
quickly and deeply 55

CHAPTER FIVE: How to know your date
even better 79

CHAPTER SIX: The next level: Becoming a
dating Jedi. 99

CHAPTER SEVEN: How to put it all together 169

Acknowledgements. 175

Introduction

I'm a fifty-four-year-old, happily married man, who has had his fair share of disappointments on the dating scene in the past, most of which I could have avoided if I'd had the knowledge I'm about to pass on to you in this book. From the outset, I want to be clear that if you are looking for a book about how to seduce to order, play the field, or trick people into liking you more than you deserve, this is very definitely not the book for you. If you're looking for something to increase your score of relationships that actually don't count, then move along, there's nothing to see here. This is a book about how to genuinely be the person whom the love of your life can recognise as the love of theirs.

In the years when I was single I found the experience hard. Not just the fact that I was on my own, although that resulted in enough lonely evenings nursing a can of lager and playing Nintendo, but more particularly it was the difficulty of finding the person who was 'the one'. I remember wandering around the supermarket with my trolley wondering if she was in the next aisle – and leaving it to chance or bad steering for us to bump into each other. I remember reading the lonely hearts but, after the first unanswered response, not having the confidence to risk the rejection a second time. I remember sitting with friends on a night out with someone they'd fixed me up with, and feeling nothing but the despair of knowing the chemistry between us was missing. In the end, after a number of false starts, I found the woman of my dreams, and I don't think it was a coincidence that it happened after I had discovered some of the ideas and research from the field of personal development that you're going to read about here. I hope these ideas can help you in the same way, because they led me not only to my wife, but also to a complete change in career, from police officer to therapist. And through being a therapist I have had the privilege of people opening up to me about what they found hard about life, and discovered it was mainly what I was finding hard myself. Our ways of coping with these common difficulties might have varied greatly, but the root was the same; it was to do with our relationship with ourselves. So this book is going to be about helping you to find a great relationship, and, as part of the process, making sure you're having a great relationship with yourself too. Because I don't think you can have one without the other.

The need for *How to Click* was highlighted after my book *Lovebirds* was published in 2012. In it I identified fundamental personality types, showing the differences in how people think, feel and act, that I believe, after working for years with couples whose relationships were in trouble, lie at the heart of why many people who love each other are unable to live together. It seems to be the rule that opposites attract, and then they drive each other mad. But it doesn't have to be so. And, of course, too much similarity can cause its own challenges, which can also be overcome. In *Lovebirds* I describe how it is possible to use the aspects of a personality that appear to be part of the problem, to be instead a source of strength within the relationship: how it is possible to transform a situation that often results in a row into something that can make a couple laugh together. What separates you could actually bring you together.

So that was couples sorted! I expect separation rates to plummet in direct correlation with book sales rocketing. But it was pointed out to me that it was all very well helping people who'd found someone, but what about those still searching?

This book is going to show you how to prepare yourself mentally for your date, as well as giving you practical strategies and the confidence to simply be yourself and, importantly, to realise that is more than good enough. But you will also learn about how to interpret aspects of your date's personality so that you can respond in a way that leaves *them* feeling understood, and create the clearest possible connection between you for attraction to work its magic.

Too often, people feel a pressure to adopt a role when talking to new people in a variety of contexts, whether it be work or social, and in doing so, they prevent themselves from connecting authentically with them. It's no different when you go on a date or begin a relationship; so often your date never actually gets to meet you, just the person you turn up as. This book intends to change that. How else can you know if you're meant for each other? I want you to come away from reading this book trusting that the best way of finding out if you and your date 'click' is just to be you.

You might be returning to dating following the breakup of a previous relationship, or have been on your own for a long time and unsuccessful at finding the right person. You might brim with confidence and be puzzled why someone you met didn't come back for a second date, or be so hard on yourself you don't understand why they turned up for the first one. The advice I'm going to give you can be adjusted to fit any situation. Whatever your circumstances, meeting someone, falling in love, and building a wonderful relationship from that, is something that this book can help you make possible. Learning about how other people may respond to the world differently to you will give you an ability to establish a rapport with them that will bring you closer and ensure that your conversations are open and understood. I'm going to teach you how to make the connection you forge with your date the perfect medium for finding out if you're soul mates. If you are, I'll help you to nurture the early days to give love the chance to blossom without misunderstandings, barriers or game playing. And if they're not for you, how to move on with your search without it holding you, or them, back.

A quick note on how to use this book

How to Click is structured as a step-by-step guide, as if I'm with you, in real time, each step of the way on the run-up to, and during, a date. However, I had visions while writing this of you sneaking a peek at it under the table at a restaurant while you pretended to pick up an errant fork. Don't do that! Using it that way is the last thing I want you to do. This book requires you to first read, learn and digest the information and the techniques provided so that you can then put them into practice. The date itself is not the ideal place to do that practice. So to start with, practise on friends and work colleagues – you'll find what I'm about to teach you will help you improve your connection to, and communication with, just about anyone, in any area of your life. If you're comfortable with the principles by the time the date day comes around, then your enhanced skills will just be a platform for creating the best possible evening.

To help you to reinforce what you will be learning as you read the book, I also provide you with the Dating Confidence Download, details of which you'll find in Chapter One. This will help you to adjust the way your unconscious mind interprets what is going on around you to create a better belief about yourself. Again, this isn't always an overnight shift, but it doesn't usually take many days before you begin to notice that you're changing.

So, chapters one to five take you through the core ideas of the book in 'real time'. Then, in Chapter Six, we step out of real time so that I can give you lots more information about personality types and how to recognise them. If there is chemistry between you on the date, then you will have the insights that will allow you to connect with your potential partner, and some tips about likely traits to spot both on the date itself, and if the relationship goes further. If you already have an inkling about which type your date is, you can cherry pick and just read the relevant sections. In

Chapter Seven I go all inspirational on you to get you using what you've just taken the time to read.

So let's begin. Your soul mate is out there. Let's learn how to make you visible to them, and how to click.

CHAPTER ONE

How to be your best dating self

Okay, you've got a date. Make sure nobody is looking and do a little dance. Now, we're going to get you ready for it so it has the best chance of going brilliantly. I'm going to talk you through things you can do to help you feel a million bucks as you walk in, and what you can do to make your date feel the same way by the end of the evening. This is going to be a dating makeover, and I'm going to start with your head.

When you think ahead to a date, how do you feel? My guess is that you're not 100% confident at the prospect of how it's going to go, or you wouldn't be reading this book for help. Confidence is an interesting emotion, because it seems to emerge spontaneously in some situations we face, and evaporate in others, and sometimes that's just when we want it most. How weird is it that you can be out with your friends and always be the confident one, and yet go to a party where you don't know many people, and be overcome by nerves? Our confidence tends to be related to context, but I'm going to show you that it doesn't have to be. Try this simple exercise. It only takes a few minutes.

For a moment, think about a situation or specific event in the past where you have felt relaxed and able to be yourself – it doesn't have to be a big occasion, just a moment that you enjoyed and the thought of which makes you smile. Let it. Our thoughts can create our feelings. Please take a moment to close your eyes and remember that time for at least a minute . . .

Now think about where you feel that good feeling in your body. It could be anywhere: a warm feeling in your stomach, a soft smile on your lips, the release of tension from your throat. Connect to that emotion and the place in your body where you feel it. Would you like to be able to feel that way when you think about going on a date, and, even better, feel that way when you're actually on it? Now imagine the physical feeling and consciously connect it to the positive emotion.

That's what this chapter is about. Confidence is a feeling you can choose, but I know it doesn't seem that way. So many people have told me humiliating tales of dating disaster, when they've been hijacked by a nervous version of themselves that proceeds to completely screw up their chances of ever seeing their date again. This hijacking happens in the part of the mind called the unconscious, which takes over your behaviour whenever it thinks that a threat exists to you – physically or socially. And if it's socially, more often than not it's going to be trying to defend your self-esteem, and it's been doing so from very early on in your life.

When we're born, self-esteem isn't an issue, because our 'self' hasn't developed yet. When I talk about 'self' I mean that sense we have of ourselves as someone separate from anyone else. New research suggests that this sense of self might begin to emerge as young as four months old. Interestingly, as this starts to happen, so too does the tendency for a child to incline towards being clingy or independent, and it's thought this might well be an influence on how confident you become as you grow up. Children who are clingy at this age are more likely to grow up to be more nervous, while independent children will be more outgoing. However, it's only more likely, it's not destiny. Overwhelmingly it's going to be more to do with nurture; what happens to you and, more importantly, how you interpret what happens to you, as you grow up. Let me explain a little about how this works, and how it can get in your way.

The software of self-esteem – and how it destroys your confidence

Your brain is designed to keep you safe. How exactly is it supposed to do that? For most of the history of our species, it is physical danger we have needed to be kept safe from – predators with teeth that saw us as lunch. So we evolved with what I call our protection response: the instinct to fight, run away, or freeze in the face of a threat. While our brains have retained some instinctual fears – for example, you may be scared of creatures that scuttle, like mice or spiders – evolution also made your brain a learning machine, with software that builds on these basic fears in order to deal with new threats or dangers which can be triggered by a specific context. For example, did you know that it takes only one occasion of a non-phobic person being given an electric shock in the presence of a spider for them to develop an aversion to arachnids? By comparison, it takes an average of five such electric shocks paired with a neutral object, like a hair brush, for a similar fear of the hair brush to develop. The plasticity and learning nature of our brains means that we can become scared of *anything*, depending on our life experiences and if the brain decides it's a threat – and believe me, that can even be a date!

Our brains can learn to be scared of anything, depending on our life experiences

So, apart from these bits of ancestral programming, our brains pretty much learn as we go, using some patterns of recognition to build an expanding and enriching model of the world.

Gemma's story

Suppose there's a little girl called Gemma, aged five, who is mid-way between being a clingy and an independent child. She is not overly insecure, but not ready to pack her bags and make it on her own in the world yet. Her parents love her, but are working hard to make ends meet and so aren't always able to give her the attention she would like. One day she paints her mummy a picture of them both holding hands. She's excited and can't wait to show her when she gets home. But, when she runs in the door, mummy is on the phone talking to her boss, who is giving her a telling off for some mistake she's made with a client. Gemma dances around her wanting to show her the painting, and mum says, quite harshly, 'Wait Gemma, I'm on the phone!' She ignores her until the call ends, then, with her head full of the trouble she's in, she's met with the full rush of a five-year-old demanding attention. She snaps, 'For heaven's sake Gemma, I don't have time. Show me later!' Gemma's painting was a representation of her love for her mum, and such love seeks reciprocation. In general, children interpret everything that happens around them as being about them. We can see that this was not about Gemma but about how her mum was feeling about work, but the brain of a five-year-old lacks the sophistication to interpret it in this way.

Children are exquisitely tuned to their emotional connection to their family, because, as far as the brain is concerned, rejection from it would be death. So the question, 'Am I loved?' is like a bee, constantly humming in the background of every child's head, looking for the pollen of positive affirmation from a parent. Much of a child's behaviour is geared towards eliciting such positive strokes. It's why we don't use up all our cute moves at once. We drip them in over the years to keep our parents going 'oh, look at what he/she's doing, that's adorable'. Then we take a long break from that when we're teenagers.

On its own, this moment of inattention from Gemma's mother is unlikely to damage the child for life, but it could make that question, 'Am I loved?' hum louder, and cause her to search more for the answer. It might cause a germ of doubt to enter Gemma's little world. 'Am I loved?' begins to demand a more certain answer, so mum's behaviour towards Gemma comes under greater scrutiny. If mum returns to her later, admires the painting, spends a happy time with her, then the hum is likely to return to its old level. But if there's a period where mum continues to be distracted, has to spend more time at work, doesn't have the energy to have happy times with her daughter, then the doubt grows.

In Cognitive Hypnotherapy events like this moment of inattention are called Significant Emotional Events (SEEs). I'm going to call them 'flashbulb moments'. Sometimes an observer of the child could guess when they're happening, other times it's so purely down to the child's subjective interpretation that nobody else could ever know the significance of the moment.

These kind of events can become a blueprint against which the brain matches present events to see if there is connection or similarity. We all have a set of flashbulb memories our brain is using to interpret what is happening to us, some positive ones, some negative. I'll focus on the negative ones for now because we're talking about low confidence, the kind that can go on to cripple your dating experiences. Suppose, for Gemma, this 'painting memory' becomes something she interprets as not being loved by her mummy. Her brain will now use this interpretation to weigh up other experiences with her. Mum not putting her to bed like she usually does suddenly means she doesn't love her, mum seeming to spend more time with her older brother means the same thing too.

Imagine your brain has two parts, the *Thinker* and the *Prover*. The adage is: 'What the *Thinker* thinks, the *Prover* proves'. If Gemma's *Thinker* thinks her mum doesn't love her, her *Prover* will interpret her mum's behaviour to support that belief. Over time 'I'm not loved by mum' becomes more and more true in her world.

Children are like little scientists, trying out experiments to see what works for them. Gemma might try being even more loving or more helpful, or might start testing her mum to see if she'll get rejected again (and be very sensitive to anything that equals that), or she might start misbehaving because children prefer even a negative response from their parent to no response at all. Over time, events connect together in Gemma's unconscious, like a string of beads stretching back to the painting incident, and the more she misinterprets events as proof of not being loved, the more ingrained her belief will become.

But of course, every moment a parent isn't perfect with their child is not going to be the cause of damage to them. It depends on the moment, on the child, and on the context. It also massively depends on the relationship over time. It's the drip of inattention, disappointment and disapproval *over time* that builds the stalactite of 'I'm not loved'. It might begin with a 'picture incident' moment, but that on its own is unlikely to create the problem. A lack of confidence is not necessarily the fault of the parent either. Just as often it's a teacher, or other children – especially their bullying.

In most people, the belief won't remain particularised as 'I'm not loved by my mother'; it will generalise to other people as well. So many people who come to see me for therapy have a lurking belief (though usually not fully verbalised), that they're not loved or deserving of being loved by anyone, or feel one of the related beliefs: 'I'm not good enough', 'I'm not worthy' or 'I don't deserve . . .'

As I've already suggested, your *Thinker* uses these beliefs to predict the meaning of subsequent events. Over time these events become connected, forming sets of memories that guide the brain to believe the world works in a certain kind of way in particular situations. If it predicts something ahead going badly for you it will 'hijack' your behaviour and get you to act in a manner that it thinks will help keep you from physical danger or social rejection. Most of us will have a mixed bag of beliefs about what is right or wrong about the world, and right or wrong about us. Gemma might grow into an adult who has no confidence in her desirability, but is awesomely competent at her job, because her brain has never connected the 'painting incident' string of memories to a work context. But let's suppose that in her first job Gemma had the misfortune of having a boss whose distraction and snappiness reminded her brain of her mother, forging a link to the chain of 'painting memories'. Then it's possible that she'd be rubbish in relationships AND have no confidence in her work. It's uncomfortable to think that life can be that much of a lottery for us, isn't it?

The relationship between your *Thinker* and your *Prover* can mean that you're likely to keep repeating the same old patterns. No wonder you often hear yourself and others saying 'how come I keep picking the wrong people?' If you do say that, have you ever thought that it's your brain's perception that may be wrong? Maybe you are so busy protecting yourself from a composite of everyone who has ever hurt you or let you down that you are not actually seeing the person standing in front of you. Let's relate that to a date.

Gemma turns up on a date with a friend of a friend. Her *Thinker* believes that nobody can find her lovable. Her date, Tom, is attentive, but her *Prover* just puts that down to him being well-mannered; he's 'nice'. Tom compliments her on her appearance. More 'he's just being nice'. He seems to be interested in her life and asks her questions about her job and her hobbies; he's working hard to make a connection. In general, people tend to develop one of two responses in a situation if they believe that they're not worthy of love. They fear rejection so either get in there first, or they look for any and every sign of it from their date. If the way we behave is driven by negative emotions, we end up with the opposite of what we intend. Let's imagine Gemma's behaviour first, as a *Rejecter*.

She assumes that Tom's only being nice and not really interested in her – in fact he's probably only after one thing

– so she keeps her defences up. While her friends find her bubbly, funny and good to be with, in this situation she's wary and distant. She's friendly, but with a bit of an edge, hard to relax with. The questions she asks of him seem to be around digging for some dirt about any past bad behaviour toward previous partners. By the end of the evening Tom has all kinds of alarm bells ringing, and no suggestion is made of another get-together. And her *Prover* is able to say: 'you see, you are unlovable!' Gemma fears rejection, so the behaviour her unconscious mind creates to keep her from the pain of not being wanted causes the very rejection she fears. And the more this happens, the more her brain will search for this pattern as one that it recognises.

If the way we behave is driven by negative emotions, we end up with the opposite of what we intend

How about if instead of being a *Rejecter*, Gemma is a *Clinger*? In other words, she taps into the more needy side of her nature, the bit of her brain that sought her mother's attention at any cost. Tom seems attracted to her, and she's thrilled. Rather than looking for evidence of potential rejection, in this scenario she deletes from her awareness any clues that he's only after one thing, because anyone who likes her has got to be better than nobody liking her. She chases him, or if she doesn't have to, moves to make the relationship physical sooner than she's really comfortable with, in the hope of keeping him. People at the far end of the clingy spectrum tend to go in one of two directions:

a) become the passive doormat of their partner, always putting their needs first, and even submitting to abuse if they've been unlucky in their choice. Or,

b) they go the other way and are the jealous, possessive stalkers who make their partner's (and then their ex-partner's) life a misery.

Of course I'm generalising hugely. We're all too complex to fit into neat little boxes, and most of us do not act at either extreme but sit somewhere in the middle. We manifest diluted aspects of one or both traits; we are perhaps a little defensive and untrusting, or a bit too forgiving of bad treatment. However, the extent to which we are either defensive or clingy will be affected by how low our confidence in relationships actually is. Who we date will also impact on our behaviour: some partners may exacerbate Gemma's insecurity, and others make her feel safer. But in a true love match, there's the possibility of Gemma healing her relationship to herself.

What's happening in your brain when you go on a date

I work on the basis that all behaviour has a purpose, and that most of that behaviour happens for unconscious reasons that often we're only dimly aware of. This is never more true than when it comes to going out on a date. Your unconscious will get you to behave in a way that has proved the best way to get people to like you, or the flip side, to keep you from people's rejection, in either case based on years of connecting flashbulb moments together. I hope to show you that recognising these patterns can cause you to believe something about your *self* – that you're a good worthwhile person who deserves to find love.

So, you've got a date, and the very idea makes your tummy go a bit wobbly. That's just a reaction from your protection system. Basically what's happened is the prospect of meeting someone new has appeared on your radar. Your brain asks itself 'What's that going to be like?' and looks back through your history to previous flashbulb moments that could be a match. If you have a positive dating history it will find a set of good experiences to match to, and it'll use them to go out in the future and build an imagined scenario about how the date is likely to go. Our brains naturally use our past to imagine our future. So if your dominant experiences of dating and relationships have been negative (or feel so at the moment), then it's those memories your brain uses as building blocks to construct how the next date is likely to go. And, guess what? It's like Groundhog Day – you keep re-living the same experience. When your brain finds a pattern of humiliation and rejection, it kicks in with the protection system that has served us well for millions of years. It will release dollops of adrenalin into your system and get you ready to run away from what's about to happen, or to freeze until it goes away, or get you ready to fight.

These stressful feelings are largely a fear of the future, of something about to happen. If you go through a period of stress (which is a consistent, lower level, protection response), your body is essentially braced for something that could go wrong at any moment. As far as your brain is concerned, something is lurking out there somewhere; whether it's a recession, redundancy, divorce, illness, or loss, something is worrying. To protect you against this ill-defined danger, your unconscious keeps you in a state of physical readiness. This heightened *state* of readiness, if sustained for long enough, becomes a *habit* of readiness, and can escalate you from stress to anxiety, and even to panic attacks. If the stress continues for an extended period of time this is exhausting and can actually lead to a collapse of your immune system, which can then create a depression to give your body some time to do nothing but recover. And it's all because your protection system – imagine it like your home alarm – has become set too sensitively and is going off, not just for burglars, but for ants, flies and mice as well. In the end, your protection system is on a hair trigger, and is set off by any match between something in your present and whatever there is in your past that your brain has decided is a worry. The result is your body treating all levels of worry as an emergency that you'd better do something about.

Our brains use our past to imagine our future

You may not have it in your general life, but if you've had a difficult time dating, and get nervous before a date, then that is why; your protection system is getting ready to leap in and protect you. Sadly, one of the by-products of adrenalin is that it shuts down much of our capacity to think – strong emotions actually make us stupid – so when you turn up for your date the dice are already loaded against you. The date turns into the nightmare your brain expected because the version of you that shows up is the one programmed by past negative experience. And this is a big point: so often potential relationships don't get out of the starting gate because we turn up, not as someone you might actually want to spend the rest of your life with, but as this alternative version of ourselves driven by our insecurity.

Does that sound like your experience? That your confidence is low because of experiences from your childhood, or because of a more recent romantic history, and your brain could be anticipating more of the same when you agree to a date – or even just go looking for one?

Now I'm coming to the good news – we can change this. Essentially, in Cognitive Hypnotherapy, we're aiming to help you change either what your *Thinker* is thinking, or what your *Prover* pays attention to. Understanding that lacking confidence is something you *do* – not something you *are* – is a big step on the way.

How to boost your confidence

I'm now going to show you three exercises to boost your confidence before going on a date. I don't happen to believe that 'cosmic ordering' or 'putting it out there' is going to win me the lottery, but I *do* believe that if I expect the worst to happen that'll put me in the state of mind that makes it more likely. I'm going to describe an exercise that is going to retune your brain to anticipate more positive dating experiences. This exercise is going to be something you need to incorporate into your daily routine for two to three weeks. The effects of it will build and build until you realise your confidence has become something you can count on without really thinking about it.

Building Happiness

Get a large sheet of paper and divide it like this:

	1	2	3
Age			
Age			
Age			

1. Divide your life into three phases that make sense to you. For example, I might choose 0–18 when I left school, 18–39 when I left the police, and 39 to the present day. Write them in the vertical column.

2. Think of three things you achieved in each one of those phases of your life; things that you achieved because of you, not because of other people. It may have been a piano exam you did well in when you were 15, a great job interview when you were 38 and learning a new language in your 40s. Write them in the boxes beside each age column, so you now have nine achievements.

3. What qualities did it take for you to achieve those things? Write them in the box underneath each achievement. I'm thinking of things like determination, stubbornness, intelligence and insight. It doesn't matter if the same word appears more than once. If you struggle to think of good words to say about yourself, it can be helpful to do this exercise with a good friend, one you trust to speak the truth. Often they'll come up with words that you wouldn't feel comfortable attributing to yourself.

4. Get a separate sheet of paper. Now, think of what you would like to achieve by reading this book; what are you looking for? Think about it and get specific.

Don't just say 'I want to meet the man/woman of my dreams'; go large. What kind of life do you want from meeting him/her? I want to meet a man who shares my love of skiing/interest in cooking . . .

5. Now answer this question: How would the qualities you've described from the earlier phases of your life help you to achieve your goal? For example, attending the language class required you to overcome your natural shyness. Apply the same determination to your date. Write down your answer as extensively as you can.

6. What can you do today to move you closer to your goal? Anything that's more than nothing is something. It doesn't have to be a big thing; for example, strike up a conversation with someone new in the office. Small steps added together would eventually get you around the world. Building momentum is the key.

7. Each night, review what you've done for your goal, and write down what you intend to do the following day to pursue it. Then look back over your day. Write down three things that happened that were good in it, three things you'd consider to be gifts. Again, they don't need to be huge things, or related to your goal (but great if they are). This morning, so far if I look back for what might go on my list tonight, I'd include

the time I've spent playing with my dogs because they came round my feet while I was typing this, asking for me to get on the floor with them. I'd include my wife Bex and I exercising in our garage this morning with the door open while rain washed away the humidity from our recent hot spell, and seeing on Facebook a friend who's been through a bad time recently, looking happy on a beach. They might mean nothing to you, but to me they're moments that increase my happiness when I look back at them. And it's only lunchtime.

This last part of the exercise is called '3 Gifts'. It has been found that it improved depressed people's moods as effectively as Prozac used over the same period of time. And you don't need to be depressed for this to work. My purpose here is for you to begin to enjoy being you more. Key to the effect of this exercise is something called 'priming'. This is a term used in psychology and its principle is, *what's on your mind is brought to mind.* So, for example, the phenomenon whereby if you're thinking a lot about the fact that you're single, all you seem to have around you are happy couples, and every film on TV seems to be a love story. With the '3 Gifts' exercise, what happens is that your unconscious learns that you're going to go looking for good things that have happened to you during the day, so it begins to tune itself to what those things might be. In the early days you might struggle to think of one thing, but as the days go by you'll find more and more as your unconscious becomes more adept at spotting them. It's a bit like Facebook statuses. I find these days that I spot funny things that happen to me or around me much more often than I might once have done, because those are the things I most like to post about. As I walk through my day, the world around me is being created by my unconscious from the things it pays most attention to, and I'm educating it to pay most attention to things that make me smile.

What's on your mind is brought to mind

Most people don't realise that we take a lot of clues about who we think we are from the environment we're most often surrounded by. I'm sure you know from experience that working in a negative office starts to drag you down, and many of you have been in a past relationship with a partner who didn't support you and remember how *that* wore away at your confidence. So it's important to make sure we get our brains to focus on the best of those things in our world, and hang out with the best kind of people because, guess what? The more we find to feel good about, the more we will feel good. If you sit around with people who are consistently moaning about their love lives, or how bad men or women are, or how hard life is, then it affects the way your brain sees the world. We feed what we focus on, so focus your brain on positivity.

Getting into the habit of completing this *Building Happiness* exercise will help to retune your unconscious mind. By deliberately and consistently focusing on the positive things about you that helped you to achieve things in your past, and by linking them to what you want to achieve now, you begin to write a new narrative for your *Thinker*. If, when you look back at your life, you begin to find the good things about you more than the things that you consider failures, then you'll start reassessing yourself – 'am I really that bad?', 'can I be such a screw-up when I've actually achieved these things?', 'am I really a bad person, when I can look back at the good things I've done?' If your *Prover*'s attention keeps getting moved on to the gifts in your life, it becomes harder and harder to sustain the negative *Thinker/Prover* alliance, and at a certain point your old belief collapses, allowing a new one, a more positive one, to begin to emerge.

We feed what we focus on

My aim in boosting your confidence is for you to see improvements in every aspect of your life, which of course then knocks on into your success at dating. I don't want you to dwell on the past, but to focus on making this new confident you the 'real' you, the person that your romantic interest grows to love. It's a thing you have to work on, but we have a secret weapon that can help accelerate this . . .

Dating Confidence Download

One of the key things I want you to do to help boost your confidence is to listen to the Dating Confidence Download

I am providing for you. You will find it at http://www.questinstitute.co.uk/products-downloads/lovebirds-resources/

The download uses a model of hypnotic language I've developed to prime your unconscious to go looking for the evidence that you're changing, that your confidence is growing, that you're in a good place. It is aimed at retuning your unconscious to focus on your gifts, your qualities and your positive past. It adjusts the way your *Prover* interprets what is going on around you to help your *Thinker* create a better belief about yourself. I want you to listen to it every night before bed. You will need to be sure that for ten minutes or so, there will be no interruptions. Switch off your phone, lie on your bed, preferably in the dark, and take several deep, slow breaths before you start to listen. Again, this isn't always an overnight shift, but it doesn't usually take many days before you begin to notice things that mean you're changing. I want you to listen to it before sleep, because that maximises the priming effect. Listen for three nights, and then, before listening again, and from then on, complete the following exercise:

Positive Differences

It doesn't seem likely that simply listening to something for ten minutes could change your mind, does it? But how many times have you heard a song that changed your mood? How often has someone said something to you and it's changed your day, for better or worse? Have you ever been told something that changed your life forever? Words have great power, and used well, they can guide your unconscious to begin to imagine a confident you walking towards a date that you see going really well, and to see that actually coming true.

Write down the answers to the following questions:

1. In your contact with people, what positive differences have you noticed that could be connected to listening to the download?

2. In terms of your confidence, what would you like more evidence of? Describe the *you* you want to be.

From this night on, write down the day's answer to question one when you do your '3 Gifts'. Relate these answers to question two. How is what you're noticing evidence of your confidence growing?

Confidence at your fingertips

I've talked about how, over the years, your brain assembles strings of memories. If there are aspects of your life in which you feel confident, it will be to do with the memories that are connected to it. As we've seen, we're usually only confident about the things we remember being successful at. Again, this is why confidence feels context related; you can be brimming with it at work, but not with your friends, or vice versa. But, actually, confidence is *only a feeling*, and there is a way you can transfer the feeling of confidence from a situation where you have it, to one where you don't. It's a process called 'anchoring', and it's based on the principle of stimulus-response. You remember Pavlov's dogs? He rang a bell at the same time he gave food to the dogs, and after a while just ringing the bell was enough to make them salivate. In neuroscience they talk about how 'neurons that fire together, wire together', that is, if two things happen simultaneously they can get welded together so that one thing can become the stimulus for the other thing to happen automatically as well.

We're surrounded by such connections. Advertisers spend millions trying to connect their products to your good feelings. If they produce an advert that makes you laugh, for example, then when you next spot the product on a shelf you'll be triggered into a good mood and be more likely to buy that brand over its competitors. You've become 'anchored' to their product. Of course, it was realised a long time ago that sex sells. If an advertiser can connect to their product a feeling of being attractive, or more worthwhile, or of being seen positively in the eyes of others, you're highly likely to choose it. 'Because you're worth it', anyone? It's one of the reasons why celebrities get paid such huge amounts to advertise products. Am I really likely to buy the brand of spaghetti that I see Brad Pitt boiling on his stove? Actually . . . yes. Because, by buying it, I unconsciously see myself as more like Brad: brothers in pasta.

So, how can you utilise anchoring to help you feel more

confident when you're dating? First, go out and choose a new perfume or aftershave you like. Then start carrying round a small amount of it in a bottle. Every time something goes well for you, every time you feel confident, every time you're happy or in a good mood, take a moment. Get the bottle out, close your eyes, focus on the feeling you're enjoying, and take several deep breaths of the scent. Or dab some on a sleeve or a hankie, so you can sniff it in front of others without it being obvious. Also, very importantly, breathe it in whenever you're listening to your download.

This is a smell anchor. Why smell? Well, smell is the only one of our senses that is not processed by our cortex. The good feelings you associate with your smell anchor go straight to your emotional centres – which is why we can't think ourselves out of responding to a smell, it's automatic. Even if I'm not hungry when I walk past a fish and chip shop, I still get pangs. To this day a particular perfume that wafts past me on the tube causes a lurch in my stomach, although the reason for it dates back to my twenties.

The good feelings you associate with your smell anchor go straight to your emotional centres

Many years ago I worked at Hendon Police Training School as an instructor. My road to becoming a therapist really began when I took charge of the unit whose purpose was to help the students who were failing the exams. They were given four weeks coaching by us, and if they hadn't improved during that time, they were sacked. As luck would have it, I'd recently begun training in Neuro Linguistic Programing (NLP), which is an area of psychology that explores how we think and communicate with ourselves and others. It gave me huge insights into how to help people learn. We developed a model over three years that increased average test scores by between 10 and 30% with less than three hours coaching, but that's a story for another book. Among the things I learned was this concept of anchoring, so when I read a report about Japanese schools pumping the smell of peppermint through the air conditioning of their schools during exams, because it had been shown to improve short-term recall, my ears pricked up. I began to get students to smell peppermint oil while they felt relaxed as they studied in the evening. Then they took the oil with them into the exam room. Their results often improved quite dramatically. It's because memory is affected by the mood associated with the memory. The peppermint triggered the relaxed conditions experienced while revising the information they now needed to remember.

My favourite proof of this is when scientists assembled in a room a group of volunteers – rugby players who couldn't cook – and got them very drunk. It must have been hard to find enough to fill a room, but somehow they managed. Once drunk, they taught them how to bake a cake. I've never found out if they filmed it, but one can only hope. Then they sent them away to sober up. A while later they reassembled them, divided them into two groups, and got one of the groups drunk again while the other remained sober. Then they were given the ingredients and tasked to bake another cake. Guess who did best? Yep, the drunks, because memory is state dependent.

So my cunning plan is for you to anchor positive experiences to the new scent you've picked, and spend a few weeks really stacking them together. You'll know it's working when you breathe in the scent and notice that it lifts your mood. Keep doing it, because, where your brain is concerned, it's 'use it or lose it'. We need to reinforce this new connection between smell and mood so that it becomes automatic. Then, on date night, dab yourself with your scent in the usual places, making sure to put some on your wrist or on a handkerchief so that you can easily access it without becoming the cabaret.

You see, the feeling of confidence is context-*independent*. What we're doing is storing up good feelings from one part of your life, and releasing them in another. Your chosen scent makes it easier for your brain to access good memories. Your positive mood then becomes like a pair of tinted goggles your brain looks through to see the world as a happy place, and you become the kind of confident person who walks through such a world. Realising that you can choose how you feel, wherever you are and whatever you're doing, is one of the biggest freedoms imaginable. It'll take some time and practice on your part, but it's well worth it.

One last tip about how to get things to work out how you want them to: *think it how you want it.*

Read these phrases: 'I hope it won't be a disaster', 'I bet she won't like me', 'He's bound to think I'm not good enough for him'. Can you spot the similarity that binds these three statements together? They're all stated in the negative. Another little rule that's useful to know is that the brain always processes the negative. If I say, 'Don't think of a blue tree', what comes to mind? That's right, your brain has to think of the blue tree in order to not think of it. It's the same when you're dieting and say to yourself, 'I can't have that cake!' Your brain just ran a simulation of you digging in, and all of a sudden you want it even more.

If you hope your date won't be a disaster, you've just made your brain contemplate that very thing, and it's going to release a dollop of adrenalin to protect you from it. You'll feel it as nervousness or fear, and that sets up your reality in entirely the wrong way for a successful date. If your *Thinker* thinks 'He won't like me', guess what your *Prover* thinks it has to prove?

Think it how you want it

Think things in the positive: 'I hope it goes really well', 'I've got a feeling he's going to like me', 'I'm good enough for him', to set your brain up with a future image of the date that releases the chemicals that leave you feeling confident and happily expectant. It can be helpful to develop an affirmation, or mantra, that you repeat to yourself as you prepare for the date, or are on your way to it: 'I'm really looking forward to it', 'This is going to be fun', or 'This is exciting'. Your mantra will start to feel true, and it will drown out the negatives.

A positive approach will give you and your date a chance to find out if there is any chemistry between you, to find out if you click.

THE STORY SO FAR

This chapter has been about the power of thinking positively. Not the version that suggests that if you just sit and imagine your soul mate walking up to your front door hard enough, then it will happen. As I said earlier, I'm not a great believer in that law of attraction, although the possibility that your soul mate will turn out to be your postie is certainly a possibility that shouldn't be overlooked. What I've wanted to get you excited about is the possibility of allowing that confident, positive, fun version of yourself to shine through on a date. By using the way your mind works to anticipate your future in the best possible way, the you who arrives on the date is in the right state to have the best chance of showing who you really are. In so many ways, we're just a story we tell ourselves, and we're capable of rewriting that story, and in so doing improving our role in the narrative. Why make your love story a tragedy or a farce, when it could be an epic?

The things we focus on become stronger, so spend more time remembering the good things about your life, the qualities you have that made them possible, focus on using them to achieve your dating goal, spend all the time you can with the people who make you feel good about yourself, listen to my download, and stack your smell anchor. We're on our way.

CHAPTER TWO

How to get in the dating zone

In Chapter One we started on the process of nudging your mind towards enabling you to be your dating best. Now I'm going to show you how your body can join in. I work with many high-performing athletes, and a buzz word that's often used is the *zone*. It's a place an athlete wants to be able to enter as they're about to perform. It's a place where mind and body are working optimally to produce a best performance. We are going to create such a zone for you: a dating zone.

Let's imagine the date's today. You've spent time getting ready. Your bed is like a modern art masterpiece, a mountain of discarded clothes; you've got through enough body spray to defoliate the Amazon, and your mirror has had your reflection in it for so long there's an after-image left when you walk away. You're ready. One last check that your dress isn't stuck in your knickers, or your shirt poking out of your fly, and it's time to make your way there.

How are you feeling? I'm guessing that if you haven't started using the techniques outlined in Chapter One, somewhere between nervous and terrified. However you'd describe it, it's the result of a calculation your brain is making about how it's going to go. But if you have been practising the exercises in Chapter One for a few weeks, there's a good chance that you'll already have noticed that your nervousness is less than you'd expect. You might even be able to call the feeling excitement. If that's true, it's also the product of that same calculation, it's just that, thanks to you, your brain has started using different information to come up with its prediction.

Of course predicting the future keeps you safer than if you just lived in the moment. It means you can plan ahead, you can anticipate problems, you can imagine possibilities. It is probably one of the most important software upgrades the brain has ever had. Now, the thing is, when you think of the future, you're obviously imagining something that hasn't happened. Imagine the moment you walk into a bar looking for your date. Your brain asks the question, 'What's this going to be like?' (that is, good or bad). We saw in the last chapter how it goes into your memory banks to find the likeliest match for the present situation. From that match it then creates the most likely outcome. So, if you've had a good measure of romantic success, you walk into the pub, your brain imagines the evening going well and you having a good time. A chemical called dopamine is released (which is the main 'reward juice' for the brain), you feel positive, and the pub seems a good place to be. The people in the bar who notice you enter seem friendly. You like how you look in the reflection of the pub window, and your date looks pleased to see you. It's all good. The exercises in Chapter One are designed to produce this very same effect – they train your brain to anticipate the positive possibilities of your date, and the dopamine starts to flow.

Now imagine you've had a romantic history dotted with pain and heartbreak. You walk into the pub on a first date and your brain asks the big question, 'What's this going to be like?' In my case, there was a time when my brain found the most likely match for that in the string of romantic disasters that began at the age of ten at the school disco, when I made the long walk across the dance floor in front of all my mates to ask the hottest girl in my class for a dance, only to be turned down. In this case, my brain had some pretty miserable building blocks to work with. If it's the same with you, as the brain foresees another let-down, it gets ready to protect you by dropping adrenalin into your system, and you find yourself imagining the worst. As we've seen, this means you're primed to notice the things that mean it's not going to go well much more than the things that mean the opposite: from the unfriendly looks the people in the bar give you as you walk in, to how rough you look in the reflection of the pub window, to the look of disap-pointment in the eyes of your date when they see you. They're probably the same looks in both scenarios, the difference is simply in the way you interpret them. And with this latter interpretation, the result won't be dopamine, it'll be adrenalin, and that's going to make you feel nervous, tense or anxious.

Anticipate the positive possibilities of your date

So with all that going on in your brain, you can see why it's so important to follow the exercises in Chapter One. We can now, just before you meet your date, add to that by practising one more mental exercise and also use your body to help boost your confidence further and get you into that dating zone. If you've had the time before the first date to stack your smell anchor, then firing it before walking in the door would be a good idea. It should trigger a release of positive chemicals and you'll feel calmer. If you've been listening to the download and doing the exercises, then it's perfectly possible that you're already feeling pretty good. But if you're still feeling twitchy, here are some things you can do to get yourself in control.

Spinning

Most people tend to think that they're stuck with the feelings they have, that if they're in a bad mood, or frightened or jealous, then that's just the way it is. It doesn't have to be. Here is a very simple technique that can change your feelings pretty quickly.

Controlling the Feeling

You're on your way to your date and your stomach is bubbling away with that familiar feeling of dread, or nervousness, or anywhere in between. If you could point in your body to where the feeling is, where would you point? (I assumed your tummy, but people feel nerves in loads of different places.) Focus on the feeling and follow these steps:

1. If that feeling had a shape, what shape would it be?

2. If it was a colour, what colour would it be?

3. Imagine you could see the shape in front of you, and it was rotating. What direction is it spinning?

4. If you spin it faster, does that make the feeling stronger or weaker? Most people report that the faster it spins the stronger it feels, but some are wired oppositely. Either is fine because it demonstrates that you can change the intensity of your emotion.

5. You can guess the next step. Assuming spinning the shape faster made the feeling worse, notice what happens when you slow it back down. You see, you can control the feeling. So slow it down even more. Slower and slower until it stops. You'll probably find that your breathing slows down too.

Essentially, with this exercise, you're creating what's called an equivalence between the shape and your feeling. Once the brain accepts the relationship between the two, what happens to one happens to the other. You can use it for all kinds of things – and it works both ways; when you fire your smell anchor and get the feeling of confidence, you can spin the shape of confidence so it gets even stronger. I use this technique with athletes all the time, as well as other performers such as musicians, actors and TV presenters, both to decrease any negatives, but also boost useful positives. And the great thing is, nobody can see you doing it.

As well as adjusting your body's feelings, you can also use it to guide your brain. The mind/body connection works both ways. To help you get the hang of it I've recorded a short download for you that will guide you through the process. You could even listen to it just before the date begins, or in the restroom during the date if you need to give yourself a boost. Just go to http://www.questinstitute.co.uk/products-downloads/lovebirds-resources/ and look for 'Spinning Download'.

'Fake it 'til you make it' works

Paul Ekman is a psychologist upon whom the hero of the TV drama series *Lie to Me* was based. In the series Tim Roth plays Dr Cal Lightman. He and his colleagues assist in investigations using their skill in reading body language to establish the truth of things. One part of reading body language involves micro-expressions – fleeting facial movements, particularly around the mouth and eyes, when a person either deliberately or unconsciously conceals an emotion being felt, and Paul Ekman is the most prominent researcher in this area.

During his research he established that human beings recognise seven universal expressions. They are common to us all, so a man in Borneo can recognise disgust, happiness, fear, anger, sadness, contempt or surprise in the face of a woman from Bogota, and vice versa. The reason this is relevant to your date is because during his research he got students to mime their facial expressions for these emotions while being photographed. This often involved them holding the facial pose for anger, or happiness, for an extended time, and they often reported that they began to experience the emotion that they were mimicking. Simply looking disgusted made them feel disgusted. Adjusting your facial expression has a direct effect on your mood.

So practise your smile. People who smile a lot are more attractive, and make the people they smile at feel more attractive. Become more familiar with your smile. Do it in the mirror. When I look at photographs I am constantly surprised at how little of my smile makes it to my mouth. You want to make sure that what you think is a happy beam of 'pleased to see you' doesn't instead look like you have wind.

Adjusting your facial expression has a direct effect on your mood

Remember what I said in Chapter One about how the brain uses our environment to make decisions about the kind of person we are, that if we're surrounded by happy people we become a happier person? Well, it seems as if our body is seen as part of our environment too, so if your body is striking a sad pose, or an angry one, our brain releases the chemical for our mood to match our body language. An example of this is an easy exercise you can do to reduce anxiety. Simply grip a pencil in your mouth by your teeth, not allowing it to touch your lips. If you try it you'll notice it causes your lips to make the shape of a smile. It would seem the brain doesn't like the incongruity of your feelings not matching your expression, so it changes your mood. Researchers found that subjects holding a pencil in their mouths in this manner while watching funny videos rated them funnier than those who didn't, and that it reduced the body's stress response during a brief period of induced stress. It sounds bonkers, doesn't it? But haven't we known this for a long time? Think about the notion of 'Fake it 'til you make it'. The movie star Cary Grant once said, 'I pretended to be somebody I wanted to be until finally I became that person. Or he became me.'

Think of a time when you lacked confidence. If I was standing in front of you now, how would I know that's how you were feeling? Assume the physiology of low self-esteem. How do you do it? Drop your shoulders, look down, and avoid eye contact? If you stay that way for a few minutes I bet you'll feel less confident than before I asked you to do this. Okay, shake that out and do this instead. Think back to a time when you were feeling confident about something. Picture yourself there. Notice your physiology. Copy it. Notice what you're doing with your posture: your shoulders are pulled back, your neck is straight, your chin is tilted upwards, your breathing is even, you have an open smile on your lips making you look relaxed, attractive and approachable; everything that is part of your physiology of confidence. Practise it standing, sitting and walking.

The more you assume the body language of confidence, the more your brain will follow it up with the matching feelings

In a way your whole body becomes an anchor for this particular state. Some people suggest you copy someone whose confidence you admire, but I'd prefer you to imagine *yourself* confident. I don't think dating success will come from you turning up pretending to be someone else. I want you to be the best version of you, because that will be enough.

THE DATE SO FAR

So here's the plan. We're at the date now, just a door to walk through. Take a deep inhale of your confidence anchor, spin the feeling if you have to, adopt your confidence physiology, now you're ready to go in. You're not going to burst through the door like Liza Minnelli, but nor are you going to walk in like you're apologising for being there. You are just quietly confident, chin up, and you have a relaxed smile on your face. Now check your skirt or fly one last time . . . and get through that door!

CHAPTER THREE

Meeting
your date

You're through the door. Well done. If you don't know where your date is, pause and look around slowly, keeping your chin up. Stand as if you're meant to be here. If you can avoid it, don't move until you've established whether your date is here or not – wandering around looking is likely to increase any uncertainty you're feeling. Spot your date? Great. Walk on over. Do you shake hands or kiss? I don't know, it's a personal thing and I'm from a generation that didn't kiss strangers, and only started shaking hands with women halfway through my life, so I'm going to leave that decision to you. If you are a shaker, or your date extends their hand, then make sure it's a firm one, and not a handful of fish fingers. Firm, but not crushing; you're not trying to prove anything; you just want the first contact to be okay. If they go in for a kiss be ready for the dreaded continental double-cheeker, but only actually do an air kiss if you're in show business or live in NW1. Obviously if they go to kiss you on the mouth from the outset you can save yourself some time and just leave. If your date hasn't arrived yet, look for where you're going to sit and then start walking. Breathe.

I called this book *How to Click* because we've all experienced those moments when you meet someone and, by some weird alchemical reaction, you instantly hit it off. If the attraction is physical, then it's likely that several things have happened, and all of them subliminal. Partly it will be to do with your *attraction criteria*. We all tend to have a set of characteristics we find attractive in other people, whether it's hair colour, height, smile, voice, warmth, sense of humour or their butt. Certain things grab our attention. And yet, just as often, we're attracted to people who don't really seem to follow our own preferences and fall for someone completely different, so clearly these criteria can be trumped. Smell is one of those things that can cause you to fall for someone without really knowing why. In this case it really *is* about the chemistry between you, literally. We are attracted to people whose immune system is different to our own, because it means that, thanks to the wonders of genetics, our offspring will have a greater spread of protection against the pathogens they might face in life. And the way we know someone's immune system is different to ours? Because we can smell it. It's ironic, isn't it? We spend billions on things to cover our natural smell, when that might be what turns someone's head – for the right reasons.

The immune system and unconscious preferences of your date are beyond your ability to influence. The only way to maximise the chances of meeting such an unconscious match is to meet enough people for the law of averages to tip in your favour. However, along the way there are things you can do to deliberately maximise the 'click' factor so that if this date is *'the one'*, then you're doing everything you can to make the click happen. And we're just utilising something that's part of normal human interaction, because aren't there times when you click with people in a non-sexual way? You meet someone and just plain like them? What's happening then, and how can you use it?

There are things you can do to deliberately maximise the 'click' factor

When you first meet people socially, if you step back and listen to the conversation, you'll find a lot of it is actually about searching for similarity, for things 'in common'. The more you find, the greater the chances of the pair of you 'hitting it off'.

It's not that difference doesn't attract. Sometimes it is the very exoticism of someone, or the promise of new experiences, that causes the heart to beat faster, but generally, despite the differences, there'll be a core of jointly held beliefs, attitudes and values that provide a springboard from which to explore each other's worlds, and which form the foundations for a relationship's longevity. It could be that you love the same music, or admire the work someone does. Otherwise, when those pesky subliminal factors kick in – you know, the instant attraction – but without the common ground, you can end up in a situation where you're incredibly drawn to each other, but just can't live together. The chemistry irresistibly draws you close, but the differences in your outlook, habits and behaviour repel. These relationships don't tend to last.

One of the ways in which we project similarity is our habit of 'echoing' other people. If you work in a team in an office it doesn't take long before you begin to form a group identity, with in-jokes, a hierarchy, maybe even a little symbol of you as a group, like a nickname. New members will take a while to 'fit in' and learn the subtle behavioural things that mark your group out as 'special'. People even start to adopt the language and accents of those around them – especially of those who are above them in the hierarchy. It's all an unconscious way of saying 'we belong together', and the power of wanting to should never be underestimated.

Mirroring and Matching

If you look at two people who are getting on you often see them doing something intriguing; they either match, or mirror, each other's behaviour. Watch them. Suppose they're sitting opposite each other, you'll often see them both with an arm on the table, or both leaning back, or forward, or with their legs crossed. If they're matching each other, then both will have their left arms, or their right arms, on the table. If they're mirroring, guess what? It's like they're each other's reflections. You know how you can walk into a pub and see two friends at the bar, and you can just tell that they're unhappy with each other even though nothing is being said? It's often because of this. People in rapport unconsciously copy each other, people unhappy with each other, don't.

I use these principles as a reflexive action with all my

clients to help them relax and enable them to open up to me. I see rapport as an unconscious exchange that symbolises that the other person is safe with you, that there's a connection. It isn't the same as liking someone, but it's a step in the right direction. The key thing, if you're going to deliberately match or mirror someone's body language, is not to overdo it. You don't have to copy everything they do, just a few of their major movements and postures. Don't rush it, transition from your position to theirs over the course of a minute or so. Subtlety and grace are the watchwords.

Creating the right chemistry

I've been teaching rapport skills for many years, and I completely believe that this physical stuff works, but it's also not the whole story. I often see people, clearly deeply connected, who aren't matching or mirroring each other, so there are other, non-physical or chemical factors that contribute to rapport and feeling drawn to someone. There are ways of being which make you more attractive to others, not just, or necessarily, sexually, that contribute to you becoming someone to whom others are drawn and feel safe opening up to. Quite simply: be kind, give recognition, be interested and listen.

Be kind

People like people who like them. Sad, I know. Did you know that if I pay you a compliment, even if you know I'm only joking, your opinion of me still goes up? And you are looking mighty fine today, by the way. We are suckers for other people's good opinion, for all the reasons I explained in the early chapters. It takes very little effort to make people feel better about themselves. When you admire the colour of someone's scarf you're complimenting their taste, and by extension, them. It's easy. Being kind makes you a happier person. Happy people are better to be around, and more attractive, whatever they look like. It's like a positive feedback loop – your brain gets tuned to fill your world with opportunities for kindness, and you become someone who lives in that sort of world. And kindness rebounds. I'm not in the least bit spiritual, but kindness rebounds. Perform random acts of kindness and your brain runs a simulation of how the person you're being kind to feels as a result of your action. Not only will you get a jolt of happy chemicals but so will they. I've always liked the idea of how your smile can travel around the world. You smile at someone in the street, and they smile back. They're still smiling as they make eye contact with someone else, who smiles back. That person is still smiling as *they* make eye contact with someone else . . . Like a ripple, your kindness and your happiness can spread around the planet. But coming back to this small part of it, in the context of your date, you will have directly affected their brain chemistry in your favour!

Being kind makes you a happier person. Happy people are better to be around, and are more attractive, whatever they look like

Give recognition
One of the best ways to create positivity around you is to acknowledge others. In the UK we live on a crowded island,

and yet so many of us are starved of contact, of opportunities to feel that our existence matters. Positive strokes from other people are units of recognition. A touch can be on the shoulder, or a smile on the tube; it's an acknowledgement that you exist in the eyes of someone else, and few people are so 'okay' in themselves, that this doesn't matter. You will find that if you make a conscious effort to connect with people around you – appropriately of course – you will emanate and attract good feelings (and possibly that dishy guy or girl you're sitting next to). So when you are on your date, engage with the waiter or waitress and you will create an atmosphere of wellbeing and an impression of connectedness.

Be interested

But perhaps even more than this, showing your interest in others is a potent weapon in your attraction armoury, and not everyone is equipped with it. Listen to people when they talk to each other: how soon do they turn the conversation to themselves? This kind of thing:

Susan: 'Haven't you just been on holiday?'

Beverley: 'Yes, I just got back from Ibiza . . .'

Susan: 'Oh we went to Ibiza a few years ago, it was lovely. We stayed in . . .' and they're off, probably for the next ten minutes without taking a breath. This trait is a big turn-off, and if you know you have a tendency to steamroller others in conversation this is something you will have to learn to be aware of.

How often have you spent an evening with friends and realised, as you've walked away, that you know loads about how their life is going, but you didn't get an opportunity to share that good bit of news you had or that worry that's been niggling. In the world of NLP, in terms of their ability to give attention, people can be ranged from *Self*-oriented at one end to *Others*-oriented at the other, and anything in between.

If you naturally focus on other people, on their needs, on their lives, then you're someone who is going to attract people who tell you their troubles, who open their hearts to you. This can be very winning, but you will need to be careful that your life isn't given over to others because it is the only way you feel worthwhile. However, in a balanced world, being able to see the needs of others, and being interested in them, will enrich your life, and make people warm to you on a date. If you're strongly down the *Self* end of the scale then there's a danger of being seen to use people for your own needs, and only being around when you want something.

**Being interested will enrich your life and
make your date warm to you**

The majority of us will be somewhere in the middle. If you listen to most people's conversations, they're a bit of a dance, where people share information and stories, where the 'he said' and the 'she said' is about even. You both walk away feeling you got something from the conversation by being heard, as well as listening. And that's where you need to be during the date.

Interestingly, if the date isn't going well, and you want to end it, withdrawing your interest can be very effective. They'll be telling you about what's important to them: politics, sport, a hobby. For intimacy to develop, generally people need to engage at the level of their values. If you show a lack of interest in what they value, or even appear bored by it – or if you really want to break rapport, disagree with what they hold dear – this will usually do the job. But remember, be kind!

Listen

Sometimes you'll hear two people apparently holding two different conversations at the same time, each one talking about their thing, and not really listening. Two *Self*-oriented people in full flow. If you watch someone on a phone for thirty minutes only occasionally grunting or managing a yes or no, guess who is on the end of the line? *Selfies* have trouble finding dates, especially second ones. Go figure.

If you think you're prone to *Self*ness, don't panic. This is not about you being selfish (necessarily), it's about where your attention naturally goes, and you can train it to do otherwise. It just needs some work. So practise paying closer attention in conversations. How many questions do you ask before switching to something about you? Ask more before you switch. Ask the person you're talking to three things before you talk about one of your own, and keep doing that until it's a habit. Remember, conversation is like a dance – you are both taking part in it. On the date, if you suspect the person opposite you is more *Others*-oriented, you may want to have some openers up your sleeve: what films have you seen recently? what do you do outside work? – just so you don't draw a blank.

All that's happening is that when people tell a *Selfie* something, their brain goes looking for things in their own experience to match it to, and then they tend to reflexively share that, rather than remain focused on what the other person was talking about. If you are a *Selfie* dating a *Selfie*, but you're the only one who's read this book, you will need to be quite assertive. Put a hand on their arm to pause them every now and again and say something like 'I know just what you mean, that happened to me once . . .' and encourage the idea of sharing the conversation. If they go on for too long and fail to respond to your assertiveness, then break rapport with them. Most people find it difficult to continue with their conversation in its absence. If you're with one of the few who can, I'd suggest an early night. Alone.

If you're an *Others*-oriented person then you'll be more naturally engaging because people tend to like talking about themselves and you'll be happy to let them. If two strongly *Others*-oriented people go on a date it can turn into a weird evening where both try to get the other to talk about themselves, resulting in silence! If this is you, be prepared with a couple of stories or anecdotes and remember they want to get to know you, so give them something to go on! Listen for how many things you're asking of them, and match them with how many things you volunteer about yourself. But, again be careful; if you're dating a *Self*-oriented person, that you are not doing it just because it makes you feel needed.

You could end up feeding their 'selfness' and chasing around their every whim, and even looking to them for your own opinion.

A conversation is like a dance

Rapport will be increased across the whole spectrum by your showing an interest in your partner and exploring more of what they're talking about by asking simple questions (not interrogating), listening to the answers, commenting on the answers and sharing ideas and experiences of your own. Women are often better at this than men on dates; I think men often mistakenly feel they need to impress, and so share lots about themselves hoping this will do the trick. When men talk about themselves it is a kind of display thing, like a peacock's feathers, only less effective because most women would probably prefer someone who listened to them.

Novel, I know, but balance is the key. Remember what I said, a conversation is like a dance; each party should leave it feeling they've got something from it, and shared equally in the exercise.

About Body Language

There's a whole industry out there that analyses body language as a means of interpreting actions – if someone crosses their arms when you're talking to them, they're being defensive or are opposed to what you're saying. I've found that alternatives can be because they're cold, or they have large breasts and their back is aching. Apparently, straightening a man's tie suggests that you're attracted to him. As you will discover in Chapter Five, there is a character type who would do that to their worst enemy simply because the untidiness was driving them mad. It's easy to make generalisations based around things like that, and we're attracted to them because they seem to make life easier. But I would be doing you a disservice if I suggested relying on general interpretations of body language is ever a dependable guide. I just don't believe that one gesture or mannerism means the same thing for everyone. Clearly, we all use our bodies to communicate, but I want to show you how to look for the particular ways *your* date expresses themselves – with their eyes, their gestures, their words and their actions. That will help you understand them and communicate more clearly.

So, with regard to what I teach about body language, I'm mainly sticking with those aspects of it that I've found will help you to establish rapport and to identify which 'Love-type' your date is. I want to avoid generalisations that could confuse or lead you astray. For example, there is the concept of 'personal space'. We all tend to have an area around us that we seek to maintain. If people 'invade' it without our permission we tend to become uncomfortable. But there could be a cultural element to this. People such as the Japanese, or others who live in close proximity to each other, tend to have a smaller 'intimate zone'. So do urbanites compared to rural folk. On a date, a Country girl could feel a City boy is getting a bit hot and heavy because of how close he's sitting or how often he moves into her zone, whereas he thinks he's being perfectly polite because to him it's a normal 'social distance'. But it could also be because this potential Country girl's Love-type causes her to feel uncomfortable if people move into her intimate space, while on the other hand, for City boy, being physically close to someone is for him a normal way of connecting to people. I want you to use body language to identify your date's type, and to make them feel at ease with you, not to make value judgements, and I'll be showing you how as we go.

THE DATE SO FAR

So, you've been listening to the download, you remembered to take a deep inhale of your smell anchor, maybe spun your positivity up a notch, and adopted your confidence physiology, before walking confidently through the door. You scanned the room and spotted your date. Smiling broadly, you walked over to your date, reaching to shake their hand as they lightly pecked you on the cheek. So far, so good. From here, it's been about matching and mirroring. Remember to do it subtly, and just choose a couple of main physical attributes, like the angle they're sitting at, whether their legs are crossed, that kind of thing. And it's been about kindness, giving them your attention and putting them at ease by establishing rapport. Now let's get to know them, and you.

CHAPTER FOUR

How to get to know your date, quickly and deeply

You've made it across the room to greet your date – a triumph in itself (especially in those shoes) – and are now sitting comfortably opposite them for the evening and have started to strike up a rapport. What's your date going to be like, and what are the signs you should be looking out for that are going to give you clues about their personality?

In order to pick up these clues, you need to be aware of the different ways people have of responding to the world. Understanding these differences can help you to increase rapport, and also to avoid the mistake of thinking that when your date responds to something in a way you wouldn't, or treats something as important or trivial when you don't, that it doesn't make them odd or weird, just different. And it means you're not doing anything wrong either. These differences can make or break a relationship from the get-go, so it's good to be familiar with them.

You will already have been able to glean quite a lot from the contact you've had, via email or telephone. Did they write long emails or seem quite brief? Did they take on the organisation of the date, or leave it to you? Did they seem quite picky, or happy to go with the flow? You will also have had the chance to ask the same questions of yourself so that you can start to build a picture of how you might fit together. In the parlance of my previous book, *Lovebirds*, you are seeking to establish whether your date is a 'ground bird' or a 'sky bird', and which one you are too. I've found that the fundamental difference between the two types is the most common reason couples don't get on, yet, if understood, it can make a couple a very powerful pairing. Let me explain.

I chose to move away from the more technical names when I wrote *Lovebirds*, but I first read about these differences during my NLP training. The concept owes its beginning to a mother and daughter team – Katherine Briggs and Isobel Briggs-Meyers. They took ideas about character traits developed by the great Carl Jung and created a system of personality typing that was called the Myers-Briggs Personality Inventory (MBPI), and which has been applied to tens of millions of people since its launch. Myers-Briggs identifies four pairs of preferences: Extrovert-Introvert, Thinker-Feeler, Judger-Perceiver and Sensor-Intuitor. For the purposes of this book, that latter pair have been renamed 'Ground birds-Sky birds'. That sound you hear is probably two ladies spinning in their graves.

Ground birds

If you spoke to your date prior to your meeting, and they spent a lot of time going into the detail of things, they are probably a ground bird. If they seemed to have strong preferences for where they wanted to meet, that's probably another clue. Ground birds like to keep their feet on the ground. They're not comfortable with speculation or flights of fancy. For them, hard evidence is what will sway them, and they like to know all the ins and outs of everything. They will also tend to have rules for the way things should be done which they take very seriously. Good organisers, they tend to excel at things that are step-by-step, and will sometimes gain expertise in a particular interest that they've maintained over years.

So, on a first date, ground birds will often be the ones who have had most input into its organisation, irrespective of who asked who out. They will tend to have things they like to do, things they like to eat, times when they like to do things, and when they don't, so you might detect a certain 'precision' in the date. There's not a lot of 'let's suck it and see' with a ground bird, and they can come across as being a bit cautious in getting to know people, a little slow to warm. They're probably not; they're just accumulating information and knowledge so they can make their minds up about a person. It may take them weeks to fall in love at first sight (and they can be prone to stay in relationships too long after they've ceased to work). It's one of the reasons why getting to know each other is likely to take time; they will feel there's a lot to get to know. Also, there are no short, quick answers with ground birds. If you ask something traditional like: 'What do you do for a living?' you're likely to get a not-so-potted employment history, starting with their paper round – a first date might be memorable for the stamina required, if nothing else. Unless they're one of those *Selfies* I mentioned earlier, they will want to know the same level of detail about their date. They probably won't bring a lamp to shine in your eyes, but it can feel a bit like an interrogation.

In the early days of a relationship, beyond the things I've mentioned, their ground bird nature might not seem too big a deal. Later, as you become a couple it will be a much bigger factor, because they will have quite set ideas about the way they like things to be, and may begin to seem a bit bossy or controlling – especially if you're a sky bird. It's easy to laugh it off as them just being like Monica from *Friends*, with her rules and need to be in charge, but it can begin to define the relationship, so you'll have to decide how far you want to let it. Bear in mind, ground birds' intentions are good. Many have a secret feeling that if they could only be elected as President of the World, they could bring about global peace. Before lunch if they made an early start.

Sky birds

If the emails you received from your prospective date were quite brief and lacking in detail, or if they seemed a bit vague on the phone about where and when the date was going to take place, don't mistake it for a lack of interest; they're probably a sky bird. Sky birds are all about the big picture. Detail will tend to bore them, and what excites them is possibility and imagination. They can be prone to flights of fancy and get deeply interested in something which they then abandon for something else that grabs their curiosity. They don't tend to be rule-conscious, or particularly organised.

On a first date, they might actually seem a bit blasé or slapdash (especially if their date is a ground bird), happy to meet up and 'go from there'. This 'not caring' can extend to their preferences for what to do or what to eat. Quite quickly they could be mistaken either for a people-pleaser who goes along with others' suggestions, or just someone with none of their own. Nothing could be further from the truth; it's just that they'll be quite happy to go along for the ride for now. If something matters to them they'll say, don't worry, it's just that not much does bother them at the level of arrangements. If you engage a sky bird in something that interests them then they'll vibrate with excitement about it and it can be a challenge to keep up with their flow of thoughts and ideas, but when it comes to responses to questions that they view as more superficial, this is likely to be what you get more of:

You: 'So what do you do?'

Sky bird: 'I work for an IT company.'

You: 'What do you do for them?'

Sky bird: 'It's kind of a change management role.'

You: 'That sounds interesting . . .'

Sky bird: 'Yes, it's okay . . .'

If you happen to be a dentist you might actually start pulling teeth for comparison purposes. Actually, by the end of the night you might start doing it anyway. It might seem as if sky birds are being evasive, or just difficult, but you're just asking the wrong questions to engage them. Ask 'How did you get into that?' and sky birds can start talking about the patterns of their lives that got them to where they are. Ask 'What is it that you like about the role?' and it might prompt them to engage at the level of ideas, and concepts and passion. Ask 'Where do you see that taking you?' and stand back. That's where they're happiest, high in the sky, exploring possibilities, not connecting to the details of a thing, or the mundane.

Sky birds can make decisions quite quickly – just not always good ones. If they hit it off with someone on the first date then they probably won't hang about in getting involved, but they can fall in and out of love in a heartbeat. If you're dating one, the falling in love with you quickly can be a fun ride, the falling out of love, not so much. It can be a bit of a rollercoaster ride with them, as they move from interest to interest, but it's rarely boring – unless you stay at home while they go out pursuing them.

Together on that first date

So you are sitting together at the table in the restaurant. You have already worked out whether you are a ground or a sky bird, and you may already have some hints about which one your date is. But if not, try this: if you ask, 'Did you have a good trip here?' a ground bird is likely to give you a step-by-step breakdown of their journey, while a sky bird will probably just say 'Fine.' If you're both ground birds, the blow-by-blow travelogue will probably spark an exchange of stories that could nicely see you through the whole evening. You might find the brevity of the sky bird a bit unsettling, as if your questions aren't interesting enough to warrant a fuller answer, but remember that's not the case, and refer back to the section on sky birds to see the kind of questions that will engage them. It will take a bit of practice. Also, be aware of the level of detail you're going into with your conversation. Watch them carefully because they'll let you know if they're losing attention – they'll literally glaze over. They find detail boring. That's detail, not you, so just do your best to reduce the information flow.

If you're a sky bird, and so is your date, then the beginning might be a little tentative as you search for something in common that will ignite you both. It's likely you'll have touched some common interests during your pre-date contacts. Once you find a joint passion you'll both go off like rockets and the evening will fly and you'll look back later and realise how many things you covered, although none in any particular depth. On the other hand, if your date is a ground bird, then you're going to need to be patient. I know that sometimes, when you're stuck with someone going into too much detail, it feels as if your soul is trying to leak out of your shoes, but if there's the possibility of an attraction here, I suggest you hold on. If your date is nervous it's probably going to be even worse. The good thing is that ground birds often don't mind, or even notice, being interrupted by a question that moves them on, so don't get too serious, just treat this as an opportunity to practise your skill at recognising differences and using them to help you get on better. Recognise that ground birds like detail, so supply it to help your date feel more relaxed. If you need to interrupt, do so by being interested, and keep moving the conversation along until it reaches a place where you're both comfortable. By turning it into a covert 'game', it stops you getting quite so frustrated while you're getting to know your ground bird.

Later, if the date is a success, other aspects of this particular difference will become important, but I'll deal with those when you get there. For now, I want the date to go well, so let's keep learning more about who is sitting across from you.

What are people to you: Batteries, or Drains?

When you look for love do you work on the basis that if you ask enough people on a date you'll eventually get a yes, or do you prefer to wait to be attracted to someone and then gradually get to know them? Are you comfortable asking them out, or do you wait to be asked (or drop hints if you're feeling brave)?

The answer you give to these questions may depend on a particularly important difference between character types which is very likely to affect how you click: and that is whether you are an introvert or an extrovert. The question I usually ask to establish this – although listening to people for a few minutes usually reveals it naturally – is: after a hard day at work, what do you most like to do to recharge your batteries, relax quietly somewhere on your own or with just a close friend, or go out and socialise, the more the merrier? The rule is that extroverts gain energy from being around people, while those same people drain it from introverts. This has massive potential for inhibiting your rapport, right from this very first date.

Introverts
Introverts like to take their time getting to know you. They'll want to do it somewhere quiet, without too many distractions, and not as part of a larger event like you and your friends on a night out. They find it difficult to open up about themselves until they trust you, so it can feel a bit like you're squeezing a stone. It doesn't mean they don't like you, only that they don't know you yet. Rocky's girlfriend, Adrienne, is a classic introvert, with Rocky bludgeoning her with his attention in a typically extrovert way. Mr Darcy and Elizabeth Bennett are a classic example of two introverts depending on nothing much more than gravity to bring them together, while the famously turbulent romance between Elizabeth Taylor and Richard Burton had at least something to do with the competition for the spotlight.

Introverts will have a small circle of friends, assembled over years, and probably won't feel the need to be in regular contact with them, but would drop everything should they call for help. They're good in their own company and can lose themselves for days in a good book. It's likely that they'll enjoy things that aren't dependent on the participation of others. They'd be happy to be an anonymous part of a crowd, like at a football match, but not dragged into an impromptu re-forming of the Beatles at a pub karaoke night. In fact any kind of speaking up in public is likely to bring on a rash. Introverts might be on Facebook, but will spend more time looking than posting, and will never poke you. Ever. Introverts aren't natural sharers of their thoughts. They tend to keep them to themselves until they're certain of their facts, or they're comfortable with the person they're with, because they're quite sensitive to criticism – mainly for the attention it brings them. For the same reason they're often uncomfortable with praise too.

Introverts like to take their time getting to know you

When it comes to looking for a mate, they'll do so from the shadows. Actually asking someone out, face to face, is every kind of scary, and they're likely to turn into someone Hugh Grant would play when they try to get the words out. I'm an introvert and, apart from the school disco débâcle, I don't think I've ever asked anyone out directly. What's wrong with an anonymous letter, anyway? Generally, they'll prefer to get to meet someone through other people – their charms tend to grow on you as they get more comfortable. They'll be the person on the periphery of the group, who every now and again drops in a little one-liner, or makes a great observation. They might dare shoot you a look every now and again, or they might show their huge, unbridled passion by opening a door, giving up their seat or passing you the crisps.

Online dating is a safe haven for them, because they can

anonymously trawl through people without exposing them-selves. They'll probably take endless looks at your profile before plucking up the courage to contact you. When you respond they may not be in too much of a hurry to meet; they'll want to get to know you first through emails, and then maybe the phone.

Blind dates are one of Dante's levels of hell for them, but they might do a speed dating event where they only have to sit and stutter and smile bashfully for five minutes at a time with someone they probably won't see again. If you see two introverts at a speed date you'll think they're communicating using their eyelashes to send Morse Code. Introverts often go on evening classes, or take up a hobby as a means of meeting someone – again, they have something safe to talk about, and the 'getting to know you' becomes an apparent incidental, rather than the main event. And their family get some dodgy pots for Christmas. It's a win all round.

Extroverts

By contrast, extroverts love to be around people. They'll have masses of friends on Facebook and spend a lot of time keeping in touch with them; their mobile bills are probably the only thing that kept the world from a complete financial meltdown. They don't tend to like quiet, so you'll see them fret on a train for a few minutes, flop around looking for a diversion, and then randomly ring round their friends for the entire journey, seemingly talking about not very much, but kindly sharing it with everyone in the carriage. Did I mention they don't tend to do things quietly? That is just one example of extroverts having a low boredom threshold; they'll always be looking around for the next source of entertainment. This can be misinterpreted if they're dating an introvert, who will find their looking around the restaurant in between conversational gambits rude, and being left for twenty minutes while the extrovert goes and talks to a waiter they went to school with, even ruder. Extroverts will rarely vote for a quiet night in, and often it can feel as if you're dating their friends too. They are happiest when they're at the centre of things, and are willing to give their opinion about anything – even if it gets shot down.

Extroverts love to be around people

When it comes to dating they're less likely to be bashful. With a social circle the size of the Arctic circle they bump into romantic opportunities far more than introverts, limited as are the latter to the fortnightly soirée at their book club . . . that's run in their living room. Extroverts will meet someone they're attracted to, make their approach, walk away heart-broken – ooh there's a squirrel – and move on to the next possibility. Getting a date doesn't tend to be their problem, their challenge is maintaining a relationship with someone once the fireworks have stopped going off. So all avenues of dating are open to them, just in the main they probably won't feel the need for them so much because a) they meet people and b) they're more open to making an approach than introverts. Internet dating won't be for them if they're looking for a serious relationship, but might be if they're looking for flings – they'll probably have multiple options on the go at any one time. Speed dating might be a laugh with some friends, those group dinner dates will be a fun way to meet new people, a blind date, why not? Because their skin is thicker than introverts the long walk across the dance floor is more an opportunity to impress with a few moves on the way than the fire walk on broken glass it is for introverts. Bastards.

Dating this Love-type

You are an extrovert + Your date is an extrovert

On this first date, if your date is an extrovert and has arranged it, you'll likely be in a noisy venue, with a 'great atmosphere'. They'll probably anticipate that the evening will be a long one, with ideas ready for where to go next, even on a work night. If you're also an extrovert, this is going to be perfect, and you will probably have a great time, even if you don't know a whole lot more about each other than you did at the beginning of the evening. This will be okay with you both, though; there's a time for deep and meaningful, and it's usually later. For now, fun, excitement, buzz and enough things to keep your attention for more than five minutes will be sufficient to get this relationship off the launch pad. It's even possible that you'll be together for ages before you realise that, on your own, you don't actually get on that well, but that's okay, what are friends for? That's right, company. I have several pairs of friends who are extroverts who never seem to spend any time on their own. They can't even have a barbeque without inviting the street. An extrovert couple sometimes has a bit of a competition going on for the limelight, and even fight over who opens the fridge, so that when the light shines out they get to be the one dancing in it.

How to make your date go with a swing. Clearly both of you are going to want to make an impact, just be careful not to overdo it. Be you, but not too much of you, if you know what I mean. Extroverts are more flamboyant in their dress than introverts, and this can also include liking to show off their assets – 'If you've got it, flaunt it' is an extrovert phrase. I don't want to sound like your dad, but leaving something for later can actually increase your allure so, you know, look dazzling but don't scare the wildlife.

With both of you being extroverts it's likely that other people are going to be part of the mix, whether it's because you choose a place that's a club or crowded pub, or because you're actually on a group activity, and that's fine, just be careful. Often extroverts can be so keen to impress their date that they spend the evening being the life and soul of the party, and actually neglect to connect with each other. Remember the point of the evening. Have a good time by focusing on your date.

If you sense your partner likes the spotlight more than you, let them have it (for now), but don't pretend to be submissive when you're not because that won't make you happy. Over time this will be a thing that you learn to negotiate about, but at the beginning it's not worth fighting over. If you notice your date making similar concessions for you, then the chances are there is some real potential here.

You two are likely to have a fun time, and if you enjoy

the same things, then it'll probably progress to a second date quite naturally. But if you didn't particularly enjoy the date, as a rule, extroverts take criticism and rejection more easily than introverts, so, if they're not for you it's probably just best to say so. In the early days of dating they'll bounce back from the disappointment pretty quickly.

You are an introvert + Your date is an introvert
If you're both introverts, things will be a lot different. You'd probably be happy for it to be in a library, and have the thrill of maybe getting shushed by the librarian. Wherever you choose, it'll be somewhere quiet without being too intimate, and you'll probably have put your cocoa on a low heat before you left. The evening will give you the chance to talk, and you'll often pick something to do to make sure there's a topic of conversation. As you aren't natural chatterboxes, one of your biggest fears will be that you'll run out of things to say, and have that awkward silence thing happen. Going to the pictures, or the theatre, an art gallery, or greyhound racing – anything that dilutes the focus off you being the entertainment, will help you both relax. If you haven't done so before the first date, there'll be a gentle searching for things in common, and if they're found, both will exhale in relief, and the talk could continue till the small hours, cocoa boiling dry somewhere, as you drill deeper into the things that matter to you both.

How to make your date a winner. Silences can be companionable and comfortable, but on a first date they'll feel strained and awkward. Be ready with films you've been to see, or something interesting you saw on TV or read in a book, just things to grease the wheels of the evening. You could even talk about this book you've read that talks about different personality types – introverts are more likely to be interested in this as a subject to talk about than extroverts, so have something interesting from it to offer. When you've found common ground then things will gain their own momentum, and from there it's about whether there is a spark or not. If there is, remember that your date will be feeling as exposed as you do by the idea of proposing a second date. Introverts are more sensitive to criticism and rejection than extroverts, so it's a risk for both of you. I'm a big fan of the notion of taking action rather than someone taking it for you, so be brave. Gather your courage, and ask them. Specifically. Not 'Thank you for a lovely evening, maybe we could do that again someday, if it's convenient to us both and not too much trouble?' more 'That was lovely. I'd like to see you again.' I know, scary, but do it.

If you're actually not too sure if your date is into you, but you're attracted to them, then you might want to be less exposed – but you should still be as clear as you can be about what you'd like to have happen next. Maybe 'I really had a nice time and I'd love to do that again' would feel safer, as making it about the experience more than the person can feel a bit less exposing, compared with 'I'd love to see you again'.

If you didn't get the right feeling and don't think it's worth pursuing, then you know how it would feel to be told that your date didn't want to see you again (if you were quietly hopeful), so we're back to being kind. Make it about you, so something like 'It was great to meet you and I've had a nice time, but I just don't feel I'm ready to date right now.'

You are an introvert + Your date is an extrovert

If you're a mixture of types, then this could be a challenging evening, but don't panic.

If you're an introvert, then you're likely to feel a bit overwhelmed by your date. Extroverts' energy levels tend to be pretty high in these kinds of situations, which increases their volume, and their need to impress. You'll probably think them a bit flash or full of themselves. Don't walk out! They're probably nice, they could be good for you, give them a chance. Remember, extroverts can have a short attention span, and can get bored quickly doing one thing – so you might find them flitting from subject to subject, or scanning the room for new things to interest you. They'll look to connect to just about everybody, from the waitress to the person who just happens to be passing your table. They're not flirting, probably, but they can seem flirtatious to you. They'll be wanting you to have a good time which, unless they've read my books, means what *they* would consider to be a good time; something loud, lively, and packed with atmosphere. They'll be scared they're boring you. My advice? Go with it. Do your best to have their good time – you might surprise yourself. In later dates you'll have a chance to slow them down and reel them in. In truth, introverts can be great for extroverts; they ground them, give them a place to 'be', instead of 'do'. Extroverts will never be happy living at your pace, so unless you want to change yours, a relationship with one may mean your partner having a life out with friends while you're at home, but if there's trust, this can work.

How to make your date sizzle. The chances are, your date will do most of the work for you, if you let them. Extroverts quite like to impress, so they'll probably throw huge amounts of energy at you. To make this date sizzle, you've got to let go and enjoy the attention. Forget about the noise of the place you're in (if they arranged the date), don't feel offended if they suggest you move to somewhere with more atmosphere (if you chose it). Remember, on a first date with an extrovert you've got to have their kind of date, and then, if the chemistry is there, you can begin to educate them into the introvert-world a little further down the line. Don't feel that you need to compete, or even equal them in effusiveness; they'll probably quite like that they are 'bringing you out of your shell', but do make sure you have their attention. If your date's a flitter, then you may need to use eye contact to bring their focus back to you; they'll probably like the fact that you're concentrating on them.

Often, the attraction you have for them emerges almost despite yourself, because there will be things you'll probably dislike – that they are a bit of a show-off, too loud, maybe a bit insensitive. This is just your introversion talking. If you're attracted, and they are kind, then trust the chemistry, the rest can be negotiated.

If an extrovert is attracted to you, it's likely you're going to be left in no doubt, and it might even seem as if they take it for granted that you'd want to see them again. They're not being presumptuous. Well, they are, but not from arrogance, it's just that if extroverts are having a good time they assume everyone around them is as well. If you're attracted, then the flow to the second date will be there for you to go with.

If you're not attracted, then there are two ways out. First, break rapport by not matching their energy, by not joining in, by not being an audience for them. Be a drag on their evening and the chances are they'll cut their losses and suggest you call it a night. If they've been blind to your best attempts at rejection then, despite your introversion, you need to say you're not interested. It should help your bravery to know that extroverts tend to get over rejection a lot faster than you, so they'll probably have another date lined up before they get home.

You are an extrovert + Your date is an introvert
If you're the extrovert, you might think your date has come under duress, or doesn't fancy you. I know this is a big ask, but take a moment and notice your date's energy: do they seem quieter than you, more reserved? Could be they fancy you, but they're an introvert and you're scaring them. Introverts take a while to get to know someone, don't share much about themselves until they do, aren't comfortable in crowds, don't tend to like loud noise if it gets in the way of conversation, and won't kiss with their tongue on a first date. Well, they might, but don't count on it. You have a choice; go ahead with the wow of an evening you have planned and hope it has the effect you imagined, or dial it back a bit, do your best to be slightly quieter than

usual, and get to know them a little. As they get more comfortable with you, you can have fun pushing their boundaries. It's good for them. It's just that you need to be sensitive. Look it up in the dictionary. Extroverts can bring some colour, novelty and excitement into the life of an introvert, and introverts can bring extroverts a sense of peace, security and groundedness. They can be awesome together, as long as they honour each other's way of being in the world.

How to make your date great. Your biggest challenge is going to be to take some time to actually sit down and talk, and to let your date talk back. It wouldn't hurt to pay a compliment (but be subtle!) – just to show that you've noticed them. You're probably more socially comfortable than them, so help *them* get comfortable. Once they are, you'll find that they are much better at having your kind of good time, but they'll need more breaks and quiet moments than you.

Don't leave them sitting somewhere to go off and have more of your good time; join them on the quiet step, because those moments can be part of their good time. Be interested in them, ask questions, put them at ease. Make sure you spend more time focusing on them than anything or anyone else around you.

If you feel a spark, and you often will because the 'challenge' of an introvert can be alluring, then arrange another date. If they say no, and it surprises you, then your homework is to become more aware of how people are responding to you, because they've probably been sending you 'no' signals for a while and you haven't been paying the right kind of attention.

If the date just hasn't worked for you, then please be kind. Introverts can be easily bruised by rejection, so be sensitive. Make it about you, rather than about them.

The sum of the differences

In this chapter you've already seen that there are a range of individual differences between people that can put a spoke in the wheel of a budding romance, without you even realising they're there. My purpose here isn't to give you a list of things to avoid when you're searching for a mate, or things to tick off on a clipboard over your first meal together. It's just that knowledge really is power. These differences can be the very things that keep you from clicking, but if you know about them, they don't have to be. When people don't click they usually put it down to their date not being their type, or to themselves not being attractive or smart enough: 'There was just something that wasn't quite right about her' or 'He was a bit weird about some things' or 'I don't think he liked me'.

Most of the time, the problem isn't with who the person *is*, but *how* the person was: their behaviour. The thing is, we all do things in life a certain way, and it's obvious that we would think that our way is the right way, because otherwise we'd be doing it differently, wouldn't we? So when we see people making choices that are different to our own, or behaving in a way that we wouldn't, or communicating in a fashion that doesn't suit us, we tend to label them negatively, rather than just being okay with them being different.

I've learned after my many relationship failures that loving someone who isn't a clone of you widens your horizons, enriches your choices and grows you as a person. And if I'd known about these differences sooner, maybe I wouldn't have failed at intimacy as many times as I did. If I'd only realised the simple truth that people are doing what they're doing for good reasons – they're just not my reasons – I'd have ditched the labels I pinned on them, and instead been able to see that they weren't noisy show-offs, they were extroverts. That they weren't narcissistic egomaniacs, they were *Selfies*; that they weren't the Rules Police, they were ground birds. I'd have had a whole new way of understanding their actions, a whole new language to discuss the differences that were causing issues, and a realisation that it wasn't about them as a person, or me as a person, anywhere near as much as it was about difference.

Ditch the negative labels and understand the differences

Just be aware that after the initial buzz of the first few dates, there is a danger that the relationship could fizzle out unless you are both vigilant. It might be that the extrovert tires of the introvert needing to be pushed into having their version of a good time, or that the introvert feels frustrated that there is never time to just sit and talk. But remember, the mixture can be brilliant. Introverts can ground their extrovert, help them focus on things for a little longer, harness their energy into more productivity. Extroverts can coax their introvert partners into greater connectivity with the world, can enrich their experiences and encourage them in trying new things. This can be a potent and powerful relationship, and shouldn't be abandoned after a few dates just because you may be driven a little crazy. If you understand this difference you can work with it, rather than turn it into name calling.

Extroverts can coax their introvert partners into greater connectivity; introverts can help their extrovert partners find peace and security

Introverts are going to like to have some time on their own, which is when their extrovert partners can go out with their friends. They're going to want some time when it's just the two of you, while extroverts are going to want to show you off to their mates. Work out how much of each will keep you both happy, and make the discussion just about this difference, don't make it about personal. Going out with their mates isn't a vote against you. When they ring at 9pm asking to come round and you put them off, it's not a sign you don't love them, only that you're past talking to anybody by then. The extrovert is always going to like the spotlight. They need to understand that their introvert enjoys watching them in it. They don't want to join them, or stand in it, period. The introvert needs to understand that deep and meaningful is barely a place to visit for an extrovert, much less a place to stay in for the evening. Whenever your new partner does something that annoys you (because it isn't what you'd do) ask yourself what this is actually about? Am

I responding this way because I'm an introvert? And if that's the reason, turn it into a negotiation, not a slanging match.

THE DATE SO FAR

So it's all going well. You're still listening to the download every night before you go to sleep and it's really paying off. You're keeping yourself relaxed and confident with your anchor, and you've been practising your positive posture and open smile at work and out shopping. Your nerves are under control so no need to spin the feelings and you're pretty certain through your email correspondence with your date that they're a ground bird. You're matching their body language, being kind and showing interest in them, looking and listening for the clues that identify them as an introvert or extrovert, and adjusting accordingly. Now I'm going to take you even deeper down the rabbit hole.

CHAPTER FIVE

How to know your date even better

In *Lovebirds*, I show you how to identify yourself as a ground or sky bird, I then ask you to establish which one of four preferences you have; do you pay most attention to what you see, hear, feel, or think? In *Lovebirds* language I call the different types Sight birds, Sound birds, Feeling birds and Thinking birds. As with all of the distinctions I'm pointing out, these are only generalisations, and most people will share aspects of several types, but I've found over the years that the descriptions are accurate enough to be useful in helping people understand themselves and the way they interact with others.

Here, I'm going to give you a very brief pen portrait of each of the four types with which you can familiarise yourself before the date, and simple ways of identifying which one your date belongs to. Then I'm going to go into more detail for each of them in Chapter Six, by adding sky bird and ground bird attributes to each of the four categories, giving you a much richer description. Chapter Six will come into its own after your first date when you will have had the chance to start getting to know each other and will have much more to go on.

The reason I want to help you identify the general category your date falls into is two-fold:

1. It gives you information you can use to increase rapport and enter their world, adapting your way of communicating sufficiently to make them feel more comfortable with you, but without you becoming someone else in the process.

2. By understanding the way they are, and understanding the way you are, you can spot how any challenges that arise in your communication, or just generally in the way you get along, are about their character type, so you don't start making it personal. It just becomes a difference you can work around or turn to your mutual advantage.

Sight Birds

They look good

Probably your first impression of a Sight bird is going to be a good one, even if it intimidates you a little. They'll look good. They might look obviously good – in that they're groomed to perfection – or they might look casually, accidentally, 'oh this old thing' good in a way you suspect must have taken them hours to get right. Their colour choices are likely to be perfectly worked out, and they'll have a sense of style – some may even have an aura of it if you squint in a dim light. I say intimidating because they often make you wish you could check your hair in a mirror, or your teeth for spinach.

You sometimes get a clue that they're a Sight bird from their profile photo. It will never be a webcam photo. Often they'll choose a formal shot, beautifully lit and soft-focused, sometimes a spontaneous one that shows them off well. It will never look like it was an 'Oh, that'll do!' choice. They'll be tempted to Photoshop wrinkles out, and maybe even use one that's from a few millennia ago, which is a bit of a paradox, because it's something they absolutely won't forgive a date for if they pull the same stunt.

They're fast
They're likely to be quite 'wired', speaking quickly, and often may be quite fidgety in their movements. They may slow down as they relax, but not by much. Sight birds take in information quickly and tend to share it at the same speed so they often seem to do everything at a slightly faster pace than everyone else.

They trust the evidence of their eyes
Sight birds will much prefer to meet face to face than get into lengthy email exchanges or talks on the phone, so while they might use online dating, and be extremely influenced by the photograph you put up, they would want to get together at an earlier stage than the other types. This could

be mistaken for pressure, but it's not. It's just that they trust the evidence of their eyes, and not much else.

They look up

As well as speaking quickly, and being quite rushed in most things they do, you can often spot Sight birds because when they're talking to you, their eyes will look upwards more often than to other parts of their visual field. Often, they'll spend a lot of their time talking to you, not looking at you, but with eyes flitting towards the ceiling. It's where most people put their eyes when they're visualising something, so they'll go there more than most. Sometimes they'll even speak with their eyes shut because they're trying to picture what they're talking about.

Also, their sentences are likely to be sprinkled with visual words. They'll say things like, 'I see what you're saying', 'That looks good', 'Do you see what I mean?' Don't rely too much on this – we all use words from every sensory system – it's just that it is common that the stronger you are in one system, the more often you'll use words from it. If you notice that this is true in your date's case, then see if you can incorporate those same kinds of words into your conversation. It'll mean you're 'seeing eye to eye', and greatly helps rapport.

They're likely to be very quick and sharp in their sense

of humour, but what will probably make them laugh most is slapstick and a boxed set of *You've Been Framed*. If you fall down some stairs on the first evening, you'll make their night.

Top tips on the date

- They get bored if things take too long, from queuing for the cinema, to someone getting to the point of their conversation. Do what you can to keep the pace up on the date.

- Compliment them on their appearance, and, if you're stuck for conversation, look around you. They'll talk about anything they can see: the décor, what someone else is wearing, or art on the walls. They'll always have an opinion.

- If you like them, make sure you don't have to rush away from the date. They're likely to measure how much you're interested in them by how long you spend in their company.

Sound birds

They like to talk
This is a reasonably easy type to spot. Sound birds talk. A lot. They get a bit of a bad press for this but they're just being them, and part of that is a need to hear on the outside what most of us can hear on the inside – our own thoughts.

Sound birds seem to need to speak aloud to know what they're thinking, so even they can sometimes be surprised at what comes out of their mouths.

They think on the outside
You don't really need more of a clue about whether the person you meet is a Sound bird beyond their talkative nature. Well, that's not quite true. Sight birds can also talk a lot, the difference being that Sight birds will talk a lot about specific things, so you'll know what they're on about from the beginning. Sound birds, on the other hand, often speak to figure out what they mean – so they tend to be quite rambly, and it can take a long time for them to reach their point, or for you to understand what that point is. And sometimes they just talk to fill a silence.

They have fantastic recall
They are likely to be an encyclopaedia of jokes, and be able to recite verbatim whole comedy sketches, often along with the different voices. Who doesn't like hearing classic Monty Python, series 1–3? All in one evening . . .

When it comes to searching for a mate, they'll prefer any medium by which they can engage verbally, so parties (not the loud music variety), pubs, or organised dating like dinner evenings. Speed dating will frustrate them – how can you expect to say enough in five minutes? They might use online sites – their profile will be longer than most – but it won't be a favourite method for meeting people. If they do join one, they're likely to progress to long emails and suggest they switch to phone calls quite quickly, so that's a useful clue before you meet. You'll need to check you've got the best possible network deal on your phone, or soon your bill and Greece's debt will be mistaken for each other.

They look to the side
Typically, when people are thinking in sounds, their eyes go to the left and right while they're speaking to you, but often this is a very quick movement which is easily missed.

They will tend to favour words that have an auditory inspiration. They'll say things like, 'That sounds good', 'I can't believe what I'm hearing' and 'We just clicked'. As always, this is a generalisation, recognising that we all use terms like this regardless of our type; it's just that Sound birds will use sound words more than most. If you think the person you're talking to is doing so, then drop such words into your sentences so they feel you're 'Speaking the same language', and notice how that increases the rapport between you.

Top tips on the date

• Give them the time they need to get their ideas out. If you try to end their sentences for them they'll only start again anyway.

- If you want them to feel good about themselves, tell them if they say anything that impresses you, or if you like the way they look. They need to hear compliments; looks and squeezes don't count anywhere near as much.

- They might talk over you, or whisper things about the film if you go to the cinema. It's not them being rude, they just don't tend to have a filter that stops them saying things as they occur to them.

Feeling birds

They're nice to be around

It's likely that you're going to feel comfortable within a short space of time if your date happens to be a Feeling bird. They tend to have a gift for putting you at ease, and wrapping you in their concern for your comfort and wellbeing. It's partly because they're usually so sensitive to their own.

They talk slowly

Early clues can be their measured speaking pace. Feeling birds are often quite slow in their speech. There can be pauses between sentences, and sometimes the sentence itself just tails off amidst much waving of hands that seem to be describing what their words cannot. If they're saying something for the first time it might take them several attempts to make proper sense of their thoughts, which is often why they can be reluctant to speak up in new company, especially if they're introverts.

They need time

If you notice this about them, it's important to pace them. If you speak too quickly they'll get flustered. Give them time and space to express themselves and it will not only increase rapport, but they'll end up liking you more. It's quite common for Feeling birds to have had a rough time at school and they can often doubt their intelligence (which is a nonsense because they're often outstandingly practical, and have great emotional intelligence), so making them feel worth listening to will get you off to a great start.

They can be passive

The way you ended up meeting a Feeling bird may provide clues as to their type. My guess is that they're less represented on online sites than the other Lovebirds, because techno isn't usually their thing, and they aren't likely to trust their heart to something on a screen. They'll usually meet someone in the normal course of their life – at the gym, at work, or maybe when they're lost and ask for directions, because they are often rubbish at navigating. But they tend not to be particularly active about searching for a mate.

Parties and get-togethers can work, but not if they're too centred on chat, as Feeling birds can get overwhelmed by words or the pressure to 'make conversation'. They'll be much happier if the talk is a by-product of something else, like an evening class, or a fun event like a wine-tasting evening, or go-karting. They won't enjoy speed dating, because it doesn't give them the chance to get a feel for the person they're talking to. Group dinner dates might work, because there's the food to talk about. It just better be good, because they aren't very tolerant if there's too much salt, or too little, or it's too spicy, or not spicy enough. That's right, you're dating Goldilocks. Bear with.

They're tactile
Feeling birds tend to be very tactile, so you might find them taking your hand from an early stage, or touching your arm across the table to emphasise a point. They'll move from a handshake greeting to a kiss on the cheek farewell with just about anyone who hasn't annoyed them, so don't mistake their touch for flirting – necessarily – it could just be a normal part of their punctuation.

They love gentle humour
Their sense of humour will vary. They may take a bit of warming up, but they love to laugh, so it doesn't take much. Verbal humour would need to be well delivered and not too rapid. The gentle humour of Richard Curtis is likely to appeal a lot more than that which depends on people's discomfort, like *Jackass* or *Kick Ass*. If they watch slapstick they'll be too concerned with how that custard pie must have hurt to find it funny.

They look down to their right
As you look at them while they're speaking or thinking, their eyes will most often go down to their right. This is where most people go to access their feelings – why do we say, 'You're looking down today,' when someone appears sad?

Bear in mind, however, that many left-handed people look down to their left side, instead.

They'll use phrases like, 'That feels right', 'I'm not comfortable with that idea', 'She's a really warm person', 'I'm getting a good vibe' and 'I'm warming up to the idea'. If you notice them using words drawn from the realm of feelings and sensation, then pepper your sentences with them as well, it does wonders for rapport, because they'll feel that you're 'really connecting' with them.

Top tips on the date

- Give them time. Often they can struggle to find words for what they're trying to say, particularly when they're nervous.

- Be alert for an opportunity to make them feel more comfortable, or to do something for them – even small things that show you're caring will be appreciated.

- They tend to be very tactile. Treat this as more a way they punctuate a conversation than an invitation. Unless it's very clearly an invitation.

Thinking birds

Of all the Lovebirds, these are the hardest to spot, because in a way they're a sub-set of the others. I don't think people are born as Thinking birds, they become them as a result of childhood experiences – either from being on their own a lot, or from some kind of unpleasantness which caused them to keep away from their emotions. This can mean that they have an underlying second preference – Sight, Sound or Feeling – that guides their behaviours, but with certain characteristics that mark them out as different. It's appropriate that this is more complicated than the other types, because so are they.

They're self-contained

When you first meet Thinking birds, you'll probably find them quite contained. They might well be charming and friendly, but there'll be a certain reserve, as if they're keeping something back. As a result they can seem aloof, robotic even, in some situations. They seem to live a lot in a world of their own, and often feel as if they're observing life more than participating in it. They tend not to be very comfortable with strong emotions – theirs or anybody else's, and so will often withdraw into their heads if they feel awkward. Talking about 'how they feel' is definitely not on the agenda with them.

They don't do small talk

Thinking birds tend to be quite deep, and they don't have an interest in trivia or talking about things that don't interest them, so it's likely that you'll either already share a mutual interest as a background to the date, or they'll search for one during your evening together. If you engage them in their interest they'll be easy company, but they don't do bored very well at all.

They are knowledgeable

Thinking birds like to know 'stuff', so they'll often have a broad knowledge of many subjects, and they like to get to the bottom of things – they don't like secrets – so there is a possibility that the date might feel like a bit of a grilling. It's just their way of getting to know you. If they're a ground bird too, they might even be giving you advice on what you should be doing with your life by the end of the evening.

They talk to themselves – a lot

One of their defining characteristics is that they have a continual conversation going on in their head, so at some points it might feel as if they've 'left' you. This doesn't mean that they're bored, just that they're talking to themselves about something. It might even be that you're so interesting you're giving them a lot to think about. The point is, we've only got one auditory channel – you're either listening to yourself on the inside, or you're listening to something else on the outside. So once they've gone 'inside', Thinking birds are no longer listening to you. The best thing you can do is go quiet, because otherwise you'll be halfway through something when they emerge, they won't know what you're talking about and they'll have to guess their way back rather than admit to it. It happens to me all the time.

They're witty

Their sense of humour will depend to some extent on their second preference, but they'll tend to be witty, very quick with puns and wordplay. Their humour can sometimes be a little sharp because they say it before they can stop it.

They look down to their left

How can you tell if your date has dived inside their head? I'm glad you asked. Their eyes will go down to their left; it's where we go for self-talk. It's also where their eyes will go most often during a conversation, although they're likely to flick between bottom left, and the area that belongs to their second preference. Also, be aware that left-handed Thinking birds will often look down to their right instead, which could have you confusing them for a Feeling bird – but not for long. They won't be looking down and talking about their feelings, or getting emotional, they'll usually be describing something.

Thinking birds tend to use words and phrases from all the other types – their second preference most of all – but often say things like, 'Does that make sense?', 'The concept seems okay' and 'A little voice is telling me . . .' If you notice they use words like this, then do your best to mirror them. That way they'll find that 'You're making sense'.

Top tips on the date

- Thinking birds are a mixture of what I've just described, and one of the other three types. Their eyes are likely to go down to their left a lot, and also to one of the other areas, more than the others. This is a clue as to whether they're a Thinking/Sight, Thinking/Sound or Thinking/ Feeling. Familiarise yourself with all of these, because it's their second type that guides what attracts them and how affection needs to be communicated.

- If they look down to their left, and stay there, don't bother speaking, because they're talking to themselves. If you don't think they've heard what you just said, repeat it. They're not being rude, they just naturally go inside their head to figure out their thoughts, and can only listen to one thing at a time. They'll feel a lot more comfortable if they don't re-emerge from their heads finding you halfway through a conversation they have no idea about.

- Find what they're passionate about. There will be something. They won't engage very well with things they consider trivial or boring, so if you're an *EastEnders* fanatic it might be a short night.

THE DATE SO FAR . . . AND BEYOND

You're coming to the end of a busy first date, where you've taken control of your emotional state from the beginning by using your anchor, and spinning to create or maintain your confidence – you might even have listened to your download during the journey (but only while you're sitting inactive, like on a train, not driving or walking on the street). You've paid attention to your physiology and embodied the confident 'real' you as you've met your date, and begun to develop rapport by matching or mirroring them (elegantly). You've engaged them and shown an interest in their replies to your questions. You are fairly certain they are closer to being an introvert than an extrovert and you are beginning to make a mental note of other characteristics they are showing. What's more, it's fun and fascinating.

Just using this knowledge is likely to make you more confident because you realise you have everything you need to be the person in a conversation who is most flexible and able to connect with others at a level that empowers you. Conversations become a thing you can control, not things that control you. People cease to be scary, and begin to be just plain interesting. If they annoy you, block you, are rude to you, or try to put you down, it simply becomes a question of 'What is it about them that causes them to be that way towards me?' By no longer making other people's behaviour about your failings it liberates your confidence and enables you to handle them – sometimes in a way that will completely change their behaviour towards you. I promise you, learning to understand others is a course you never graduate from, but one that never bores you.

So, in a way, working to have a better dating experience is just a microcosm of working to make the rest of your life better too. But let's get back to the business at hand.

Ending the first date

It's the end of the first date. How did it go? Did they seem interested? Use the guidance about rapport if you're not sure. Did they look as if they were trying to engage, or were they looking away? Did they respond to your matching and mirroring, or did they break it? Usually you can tell from their level of engagement whether someone's attracted to you or not, but if you have any doubt, and you want to see your date again, then take action yourself – and ask. It's much more empowering (and less damaging to your confidence) to be active rather than to sit and wait to see if they ask you. Introverts are always going to be more circumspect in this area than extroverts, so don't mistake reticence for reluctance. If you've had a good time then actually say so, don't hint at it. If you say 'This is a nice place, I'd like to come here again', some people will understand this is a clear hint that you mean with them, but some will remain oblivious to anything less than a printed invitation, so be clear.

If nothing has clicked with you, or the date just hasn't been going well but you don't feel assertive enough to say anything, breaking rapport can be a kind way of getting the message across. When they lean forward, lean back, and vice versa, and don't match their movements. It becomes incredibly hard to keep going in the face of such an absence of encouraging signals. Perhaps it's where the phrase 'cold shoulder' came from – a turning away to indicate a lack of physical connection. But leave your date feeling as good as you're able to, because we all know that, for most people, it sucks not being fancied by someone you are attracted to.

Be kind. One of the most damaging effects of 'not clicking' is when it feels like a judgement against you as a person. So don't say 'I don't feel anything between us', as it's pretty hard not to take that personally. Making it about you is probably the easiest way to end the evening well, and without hurting your date's feelings unnecessarily. Try something like this: 'This evening has been nice, and it's made me realise I'm not ready for a relationship yet', or 'I've enjoyed myself, and I think I need to sort my head out a little before I get into something'. Notice also how I used 'and' instead of 'but'. 'But' cuts off what comes before it, so the compliment is wasted, while 'and' keeps both halves part of the meaning of the sentence. Whatever you do, don't pretend to have had a good time, and agree to repeat it if you don't intend to (which is most common with introverts). It's always better to get an unpleasant thing behind you than live with the future prospect of it. Give a kind reason, shake hands rather than kiss their cheek, and leave.

If you have clicked, I leave it to you how the evening ends. I'm not your dad, remember? But, then again, the pyramids probably wouldn't have lasted as long as they have if they'd rushed the foundations. If you're looking for a lasting relationship, there's no need to rush anything. If your date asks you out again the next night and you're not available, that's okay, just explain openly. The love you're after, lasts, so don't grab at it. That was a bit like I am your dad, wasn't it?

And I probably don't need to tell you not to play games now. If you want this relationship to work don't play cool and wait to text them, or leave it a few days before you ring. Be kind and give yourself over to the potential of this relationship like you've never been hurt, and nobody has ever let you down. Show them through your actions and your words that you're interested. If you've had a nice time say so, but don't gush. Keep it light, for example 'I had fun'. We can never control what others do, but we can control what we do. So do what you think is being the best version of yourself. Be authentic. Sure, sometimes people will hurt you because you've been open, but not as badly as your life will hurt if you stay closed.

CHAPTER SIX

The next level: Becoming a dating Jedi

In this chapter I'm going to give you even more detail on the different personality types to help take you through the early weeks of a fledgling romance after the stunning success of that first date. Then you need to buy *Lovebirds*. That will see you through to the long term. Ideally, you will have familiarised yourself with what's coming up long before your date. We are going to be looking at eight 'Lovebird types'; specifically, ground/sky birds with sight/sound/feeling and thinking preferences. Here they are:

	Sight	Sound	Feeling	Thinking
Ground bird	Peacock	Robin	Swan	Kingfisher
Sky bird	Swift	Nightingale	Dove	Owl

If you're not sure of your type, or your date's, then there is a quiz you can take at www.lovebirdsbook.com. My suggestion

is that, when you progress to an actual relationship, you put
this under your new partner's nose so they become as good
at understanding what you're looking for as you are at understanding their needs.

Swifts

I'm lucky to live in a house where the surrounding sky is
filled in the summer with these beautiful birds, which cease-
lessly soar and swoop, never resting, constantly chittering
to each other, and seeming to place as much importance
on how cool they look in flight as on the direction they're
going. They're sky birds – what else – and in their agile
flight, respond strongly to what they see. Their human coun-
terparts are much the same.

Looking for love: how to click with a Swift

Swifts should never, ever, go on a blind date. Ever. They,
probably more than any other type, are most prone to
falling in love at first sight. So what's the danger of a blind
date? They can make up their mind in a heartbeat, just
based on a look as they walk into a room. It'll take a few
minutes longer to decide whether or not someone is a soul
mate, but they'll be clear on whether the person they're
looking at from across the room is a yes or a no. And if
it's a no, the rest of the evening is a bust – it's unlikely
that the date will recover from a negative first impression.
I'm not suggesting that Swifts are superficial, it's just that

they base decisions so very strongly on what they see, and trust those decisions even when they're made in a split-second. If it sounds odd to you, it's just a trait that you don't share.

Online dating is a good idea for Swifts, because it gives them an opportunity to peruse photos and make those kinds of snap judgements before actually meeting anyone, which avoids a lot of hurt feelings. If you were watching over a Swift's shoulder you'd probably be amazed just how quickly they can scroll through pictures, separating yeses and nos in seconds – hence the 'being hit with cupid's arrow' propensity. For them, as attraction can be so instant, they often interpret it as being more meaningful than it might actually turn out to be.

If you're going on a date with a Swift, we'll assume you've passed that first test, which is not inconsiderable – so go you! As I mentioned just now, if you've connected through a dating site, I'm just hoping now that you didn't Photoshop your picture or send one in that was from a few years or 20lbs ago. That sound you heard in the pub while you were looking in your bag? It was the door closing behind your date as they left. Represent yourself honestly, because who else can a potential partner fall in love with other than the person they meet? But be ready for them to have tweaked their own picture. Swifts allow themselves their little deceits, but you won't be allowed the same. Of course, if you're both Swifts, and both do it, it'll be the shortest date in history!

It sounds obvious, but how you look is going to matter. It doesn't mean that you have to change your style or over-dress, just that you look as if you've clearly put some thought and attention into your wardrobe choice. Swifts (in fact all Sight birds) equate how you look with how much you care. It's a complaint I hear from them regularly, 'He just doesn't make an effort any more', or 'She's let herself go.'

Swifts will like to share experiences they can talk about afterwards, so don't be surprised if they suggest the pictures, an exhibition, or a trip to the zoo as a first date. If you're going for a meal, then a place that's visually interesting will be a good choice – even if it's because of the naff memorabilia on the walls. Swifts are stimulated by what they see, so while a dimmed alcove might seem a cosy choice, it could reduce their enjoyment; it's not that you're not enough, but Swifts pay most attention to visual stimuli.

Après first date

Early dates are likely to be quite long. Swifts tend to have a lot of energy and often don't need that much sleep, so if your date is enjoying your company (and is not heavily introverted) they'll be happy to extend the evening until it's the morning. If that doesn't suit you, or isn't possible, then make sure you say, so that your need to get away is not misinterpreted as a lack of interest. Swifts can get intense quite quickly and may try to move the relationship along faster than you're comfortable with, so, again, make sure you remain in control of your choices – they are not intending to pressure you, or thinking that you're easy, just assuming that you move at the same speed they do; the mistake everybody tends to make.

As the relationship progresses a Swift will want to spend a lot of time with you. If you're the kind of person who likes to retain some time for yourself, this might seem a bit needy or clingy. It isn't, it's just another thing Swifts weigh affection with. If you're choosing to spend time doing something else – say, going to a book club – when you could be spending it with them, they may conclude that you prefer that activity or those people, to them. You can't keep a Swift happy with a quick text or email, only face to face will count (although Skype will probably give you a bit of breathing space). One of the ways they know they're loved is by the looks you give them, so it's not surprising that being face to face with you is so important. Remember, to a Swift the equation is quite simple: Time = You Care. So you're going to have to give time to the relationship if you want it to go anywhere.

Giving and receiving gifts is a big deal for Sight birds more than it is for most other Lovebirds – and there's a fair chance a Swift will have bought you a gift on the first date. Swifts will mark occasions, send cards, surprise you with an anniversary – even though you might think that going out for a week doesn't warrant it! Often they'll spend a lot of time on matching the present to the person. Receiving presents means a lot to them too, so if you have an inkling that they might be a Swift, bring a little gift with you on the date. That doesn't mean expensive, just be a little imaginative. Give them the gift receipt though and don't take it hard if they swap it for something else! It'll take time and practice to hone your talent for gift-buying for a Swift – if you're not a Sight bird too they have a head start, they've been working on it since pre-school – but don't worry, you'll probably end up enjoying the challenge.

As I mentioned in Chapter Five, one of the first things you may notice about Swifts is that they'll have a 'look'. It might not be high fashion, but it will be a deliberate style. They often have a fantastic sense of colour and can make unconventional choices really work. They're more likely to have an eclectic sense of style, both in personal and home décor, than their Peacock cousins.

One of the next things you'll notice is their pace. Swifts take information in very quickly, and tend to communicate it in the same way, so being with them can be a bit of a whirlwind, as they jump from subject to subject. They speak quickly, and can get impatient with people who don't, even finishing their sentences for them in extreme circumstances. Like all sky birds they're great starters at things, not necessarily so hot at seeing something through if they begin to lose interest in it, so be ready for them to have sudden passions for things that then wane. I'm afraid sometimes that can include their relationships. The best way to avoid this is to dive into their passions with them; they'll be looking for a soul mate to explore the world with, someone who wants to be with them in every-thing, not someone who does their own thing while they do theirs.

As a sky bird, Swifts hate detail. It won't take long to discover that. They just don't pay attention to the minutiae of life, so will often repeat the same mistake, overlook important details, and forget stuff. They might love the idea of being organised, but never quite get around to becoming so. I remember giving a Swift a Filofax for Christmas and how excited she was over the possibilities it offered to finally 'sort her life out'. Six months later it was still in the cellophane. I'm not saying that it's okay for them to abdicate responsibility for making things happen, but if you do leave it to your Swift to organise your night out, be ready for some important step to be missing. I've heard many tales of missed flights because of forgotten passports or date mix-ups, of losing money over missed credit payments, even of losing a house sale because of an overlooked detail. In the early days of dating, expect them to turn up at the wrong place, or on the wrong day, or without their trousers on. Just bear it in mind and, with arrangements, keep an eye on how things are going and don't leave to the last minute your checks on anything essential, especially if it stresses you out.

'Why?' is a big word for Swifts. Unless they can see a reason, they probably won't comply with any instruction they're given – and while I'm on the subject; if you ever get to the point of moving in together, you can probably forget them ever reading instructions on how to assemble flat-pack furniture. Swifts 'work out' how to do stuff like that, even if it takes longer, ends up a bit wobbly, and has some bits left over. They tend to be quite laid back about most things that aren't to do with how things look, so while they'll have any number of ideas about what should be worn with what, in the rest of their life they can appear quite chaotic. If you're someone who likes rules, then you've got a job on your hands. It's not that they ignore them deliberately, it's just that their attention will be on something else and they just won't notice that now is the moment when your rule should probably kick into action.

Swifts in a nutshell
- Visual
- Like to look good
- Like you to look good
- Do everything at a fast pace
- Need face-to-face time
- Not strong on detail or organisation
- Tend not to comply with 'rules'
- Know they're loved by the looks you give them, the amount of time you spend, and the gifts you buy

How to click if we're the same
- Always double-check arrangements with each other
- Remember that you may both be intense quite quickly, so try to keep one foot on the ground, and don't abandon your friends in the heat of your new passion
- Don't get competitive over taste, or who outshines the other

How to click if we're different
- Set aside a little more time than you might normally do so that you can spend time together, perhaps join in with one of their interests
- Get into the habit of looking out for small gifts that describe them perfectly

- Compliment them on their appearance, and always be alert for any new outfit or change of style
- Surprise them with trips to see something exciting, like the theatre, an exhibition, or a film they'd like

Let's talk about sex, baby

As your relationship deepens, sex is obviously going to become an important aspect of it. As you'd expect, what turns Swifts on is visual stuff. They'll have certain things they'll like you to wear that will turn them on – listen to the compliments they give you, they're probably the biggest clue. More than other types they might have strong preferences for a particular part of the body; they'll be a 'leg man' or a 'butt woman'. This can be a pressure for Sight bird partners, as Swifts expect them to continue to fit the template. If they take a photograph of you on an early date, it's almost as if they're freezing you in time. This is what they signed up to, this is what they expect, so they can be unsympathetic to weight gain, and don't even think of a hairstyle change without consultation or you'll get major pouting. What you need to remember is that it is their type that is driving this, not that they are a control freak. And knowing this, if it annoys you, it's easier to talk about it.

Swifts can be very quick to be put in the mood for the smoochy stuff, because they respond so quickly to visual stimuli, so a look, or clothing you appear in that they like, can be all it takes. While they'll enjoy a day of building the sexual tension with flirty naughtiness, quickies will also be a big part of the scene – which is a compliment to you; if those diminish there's usually a reason.

Role play can be fun for them, so if you have a local fancy dress shop, get them to start a loyalty card scheme, and be ready to be greeted at the front door by Jack Sparrow or Cat Woman, but don't bring the boss home for dinner without a phone call ahead. With the sex itself, they'll probably enjoy looking at your face to see the pleasure they're giving you (so you might want to check your sex-face in the mirror) and positions that allow them to enjoy the view – for the man from behind or beneath, for the woman on top or beneath – are likely to be favourite. Lights are obviously going to be on, always, and don't forget mirrors as an option. Later in the relationship, if you're up for it, filming yourselves might be a real turn-on for them, because porn is often a favourite way of getting them in the mood, so what better than your own efforts?

Peacocks

As a Sight bird, what Peacocks see is all important to them and they share many of the same characteristics as Swifts. However, the big difference is that they are ground birds, so like to be equipped with all the facts before making decisions, and rules are likely to be important to them.

Looking for love: how to click with a Peacock
Peacocks are unlikely to ever go on a date with a stranger, sight unseen. They'd want to be sure there was an

attraction beforehand, because if the sight of you didn't spark the fires of romance in their heart, they'd see little reason to continue the date. Online dating is by far the best option for them, so they can do their dismissing in private, and scroll through hundreds of possibilities at a rate that would upset you if one of them was you. And, if you're registered on an online site, it may well have been. Group dinner dates, or speed dates are okay too, because they can easily move on without awkwardness.

If you're meeting up where the only view of you has been through a photograph, please make sure it's a good representation of you – no Photoshopping, soft lenses, lucky angle or pulled from your archive. It needs to look like you now, or they'll feel cheated and you're off to a bad start. Or an early finish. Unfairly, they'll sometimes do that themselves; they can be very vain.

Unless you're a ground bird too, it's likely that· they'll have done the organising for your first date. They tend to be happier if they're in control of situations and will feel more comfortable knowing how the date is going to go. They like to have a plan. Also, they tend to have strong preferences for things, which might include types of food, favourite bars or types of films, so an unnecessary tension is avoided if they're in control of the choices – as long as you're happy with the range those choices offer. If you're both ground birds you'll soon spot that you're both trying to take charge, and it's just going to take a conversation to sort out what would work best for both of you.

On the date itself, Peacocks will have obviously dressed to impress. That's not to say that they'll look like Lady Gaga or Gok Wan, but they'll have looked long and hard in their mirror – and several reflective surfaces since – and been happy with the result. Appearance is something they'll never leave to chance. Neither should you, because how you look will be interpreted as how much you care about the date. I'm not suggesting you doll yourself up beyond what you normally would, or dress as somebody you're not – that's the very last thing I'd want – but show from your choice of clothes that this date is important to you, not just a 'rushed straight from work' kind of casual.

Peacocks like detail, so be ready to answer lots of questions, and go deeply into any subject that comes up. Also be ready to hear a blow-by-blow narrative of their life too. There are no short cuts with ground birds, they need to know lots about you to feel they know you, and they'll assume you need the same. If you don't, keep nodding while they tell you and write a novel in your head. You'll also probably start noticing their rules too. There will be 'ways' of doing things, from stirring their tea, to hanging their jacket, to where they keep their keys. Order is very important to them, and rules are their way of maintaining it. In general, with ground birds there is an unspoken belief that the world would be better if everyone else followed their rules too, so partners can sometimes (I mean really often) feel as if they're being 'improved' by 'helpful' sugges- tions, 'thoughtful' guidance and 'gentle' nudging towards a change in your ways. This may even begin on the first meeting. It's a bit like trying to make a glacier take a break; they will never give up until you're their version of the best you could be – and, if you get into a relationship with them, make sure you fall short of their ideal, or they'll leave you in search of a new partner to polish. And I'm not really joking; you need to be a 'work in progress' for the length of your time together. Understanding that this is just their way, and they'd do it with anyone, means that there's no need to take it personally, or for it to erode your confidence. This is about them trying to polish the world into their version of it. Respond to anything they say that you find valid, and ignore the rest. My wife is like this, and in the early stages I used to take it personally and get defensive. Then, when I realised what it was about, it became something I would joke about, and call her 'little madnesses'. That was a mistake because she was acting from a positive intention, and I was then making it personal against her. Now, I keep my smiles to myself, do my best to honour her intention (to make our life better) and not bend to anything that goes against what I feel is important to me. Which, being a sky bird, isn't much. And she swears she doesn't do it as much . . .

There are certain key ways Peacocks will know that you care, and it'll be the same way they show that they care. The first of these is time. For Peacocks, time has a weight. If you put how much of it you spend with them on their scales it will show how much you care for them. So your new relationship could get quite involved, quite quickly. They're likely to want to see you a lot, move to spending weekends together from very early doors, even talking of going on holiday by the end of the first evening. Some people will feel that they're being pressured or rushed – or that their date is only after one thing. What time is for them is an act of caring; it is a currency and they want to spend it on you, and they want to see you chipping in too. If it all feels too fast then say so, but make sure you say it in a way that reflects your understanding of what they're trying to communicate to you.

Après first date

When a relationship develops, the need to see you is going to be an ongoing challenge – Peacocks are the kind who turn up at your work to take you for a surprise lunch, or plan to whisk you away for an intimate weekend without checking with you about your own commitments. If there is any tendency towards insecurity it will show in the way they interpret your spending time away from them as a sign of your feelings for them. If work suddenly requires you to do longer days, they may start to sulk. If you started dating during the close season for your sport and suddenly start needing to do pre-season training, they might start asking you who you prefer, them or your team mates? Time is always going to be a thing you'll be counting up in your head to make sure you're spending enough on them. It's a thing for you both to be aware of, and probably an ongoing subject of negotiation so they don't feel neglected, and you don't feel pressured. And, of course, if you can talk about it and help them to understand that it's just the difference between you, it can take the heat out of the situation and make it easier for you both to be accepting.

Time isn't the only thing you'll be spending – gifts are another currency of affection. Peacocks are likely to regularly give you presents of various sizes and values, sometimes to mark a special occasion, more often just to show that they were thinking of you in the moments you weren't together. They're usually very good in their choices, and the longer they know you, the more true that will be; they'll rarely saddle you with toot. What's good for the Peacock's partner is good for them too, they'll love it when you surprise them with something – again, it doesn't have to be expensive, it just has to say. 'I get you.' You'll spot your early mistakes – in charity shops, mainly – but as time passes you'll begin to see opportunities. Take them. Whoever said 'it's the thought that counts' wasn't a Sight bird. It's the gift that arose from the thought that counts.

A lot is communicated by a look. Peacocks will have lots of them, intended to communicate more than words could. They'll have an 'I love you look', which I hope you get to see, as well as an 'I want you now' and a 'Fancy this for tea?' look. Make sure you don't get those two mixed up; supermarkets have no sense of humour. Peacocks will be looking to learn your looks too. If you're a poker-faced individual this could make things harder for you as a couple, as they'll lose a major way of synching with your mood. Do your best to relay your feelings through your face. Also, if I can return to clothes for a moment, Peacocks look on you kind of as an extension of themselves, so when they look at you, they're assessing what the world will think of them with you looking like that. It can mean that they are quite forth-coming at giving you . . . let's call it feedback. If they're being diplomatic they might say, 'I'm not sure that's quite the right colour for you.' They mean, 'Really?!!!!' If they're more forthright, they'll just say. 'Not with me you're not.' You need to be robust in defence of your own choices, or surrender and let them dress you if it doesn't matter to you. You'll look great in the eyes of the person for whom it matters, even if not in your own. As you can see, this is a common area of discord in couples containing a Peacock, so it's important that it becomes an item for discussion in your relationship, don't just let it nag at you.

I mentioned earlier that Peacocks might seem to be fast movers when it comes to progressing the relationship, and that's only part of it. They tend to move at pace in most things. They tend to be early risers – once they're not teenagers – and wake up without a warm-up, so if you're one of those people who can't talk until after their second cup of coffee, you'll need to keep away from sharp objects so you don't do Peacocks damage. Just remember to be tolerant; they're not doing it to annoy you and, with any luck, you can train them to bring you a cuppa in bed – either that or suggest an early morning task, like a paper round. As a result of having lots of rules they'll always find things that need to be done, so sitting still can be a problem for them; they'll be forever popping up while you're watching something on the telly, and then asking what happened when they come back. They will go into the nuts and bolts of everything, so often talk at great speed so they can fit into daylight hours everything they want to say. Kicking back is not a thing they do easily.

Peacocks in a nutshell
- Visual
- How they look, and how you look, will matter to them
- They have rules, and breaking them is seen as a sign of not caring for them
- They like hard facts and evidence rather than trusting gut instincts
- They go into detail for everything
- They like to do things quickly. Going slowly at anything will drive them mad
- They like to be in control and organise things
- They know they're loved by the amount of time you spend with them, the gifts you buy them, and the looks you give them

How to click if we're the same
- Work out what rules you have, which ones you share, which ones contradict or impact on each other negatively, and find a compromise
- Remember to try new things. Sometimes you can settle too quickly into a rut
- If you can find a common interest you'll have a lot of fun pursuing it
- Don't get competitive over taste, or who outshines the other

How to click if we're different
- Their rules are important to them. Find out what they are and do your best to honour them
- If some of those rules impact on your happiness, make

sure to have a conversation about them, don't bend to them, or break them for the hell of it

- Stimulate them visually with trips and dates that will excite or interest them
- Compliment them regularly on their appearance and make sure you notice any change they make to their appearance or to their home

Let's talk about sex, baby

Peacocks will get turned on by how you look, and they'll tend to have very specific ways they like you to look for that purpose: favourite styles, outfits and fantasies. They'll often gravitate to a 'type', from hair colour to various other physical attributes. I've known a number of Peacocks who left their partner for someone else, and when I met them they looked very similar to their former partner (just usually younger). This is a little bit of the tyranny that can accompany being with a Sight bird; they're very sensitive to physical change. Who they fall for is who they want, so if you add or subtract some pounds, and no longer fit their template, you'll probably notice their attention flagging.

On the plus side, they picked you, so you *are* their type, and your looks can be a potent way to turn them on. Learn the look that gets their engine revving, the parts of your body they love the sight of most, and tease them with them – in private, or in public if that's what you both like. Sexting with naughty photos can be the prelude to a great evening when you get home. They're certain to like the lights on to best see you. They'll probably be quite intent on your face, because they get to see the pleasure they're giving you. Mirrors can be a great sex aid, as can cameras – but I wouldn't suggest them the first time you sleep together; slow down cowboy, and build some trust first.

Peacocks – especially men – will enjoy having oral sex performed on them, because it looks hot. Women are likely to like their breasts kissed for the same reason. Giving oral sex might not be a favourite activity, because the view isn't that great. If this is an issue for you, then talk about it and be sensitive. Be creative and see how you can make it better for each other. We all enjoy different things, so whatever you do, don't take it personally. For men, doggy style can be a real turn-on, because there's lots to see, and being underneath tends to work for them too. For the ladies, underneath or on top gives a similar view. Many Sight birds take the visual stimulation to the next level, enjoying role play and dressing up. Who hasn't got turned on by their partner dressed as Lily Savage? Oh . . . okay, moving quickly on. Whether you go full tilt by meeting in bars as strangers from a famous film, or pull the curtains and re-run *Pretty Woman* in the privacy of your own home, obviously doesn't matter, just as long as it's a turn-on for both of you, or at least not a turn-off for either.

Nightingales

Have you ever asked someone a simple question like 'Where's the toilet?' and got a rapid-fire response as though their mouth's some kind of verbal machine gun? If you have, you're probably talking to a Sound bird. Sound birds use the world as a sounding board. Half the time they're talking at you, rather than to you, at least while they order their thoughts. Once they have, the conversation normalises, until they next need to work out what they're thinking. If you've ever seen two people who seem to be having two different conversations with each other, at the same time, and neither seems to notice or care, then they're probably Sound birds.

Looking for love: how to click with a Nightingale
Nightingales are likely to meet people through a variety of means – like friends desperate to stop them whingeing for hours on end about being alone – but a thing that will distinguish a Sound bird is that they'll almost certainly need to speak to their date before meeting them. They'll want to hear their voice, and they'll want to get a sense of them through conversation.

Nightingales can be tremendously sensitive to voices and accents. I know of one who, when he spots a woman he likes the look of in a bar, uses the approach line: 'Excuse me, have you seen a big ginger-haired bloke come in here? I was supposed to meet him.' It's a completely made-up line, and its sole purpose is so that he can hear her voice. If he doesn't like the sound of it he just thanks her and walks away. If her tones are sufficiently dulcet to his ear, he'll proceed with something like, 'He is so unreliable, he's left me on my own in pubs loads of times because he changes his mind. Oh well, my name's Ian . . .' and he's into his Sound bird patter. Which is often very smooth, amusing and charming. At least for the first couple of hours.

On a first date, clearly, the opportunity to talk is going to be paramount, so the format of the date itself is probably going to be quite simple. There's little point in doing an activity date, like going to see a movie, because they'll probably talk all the way through it, but as a companion-date for a wedding Nightingales are a complete bust. They will want to tell you everything, all in one go. They'll probably also want to hear a lot about you, but not necessarily straight away, not because they're selfish, but the excitement of meeting you, the amount of stuff going on in their heads, and their hope of impressing you could just turn them into this word-tsunami. They'll settle down later, I promise.

Nightingales are sky birds, so detail isn't important to them. Their conversations will roam over a great range of subjects, often in a very short space of time, but without going deeply into any of them. They'll love skimming over new ideas, going over old film and TV shows – they're the kind of people who can regurgitate whole scenes – and are often very into music. The music you have on your iPod will have more significance than you can possibly know, and they can be tremendously snobbish about what is acceptable music, and what isn't. And anything that comes from *Britain's Got Talent,* or Justin Bieber's lips, isn't. That date will only go in One Direction.

If they don't play an instrument themselves, they're likely to be quite invested in certain artists, so finding out who those are – and having a listen if you're not familiar – is a good idea. They'll enjoy pointing out lyrics that have a special meaning, be moved to tears by a piece they find particularly meaningful, and can often sing a song in its entirety after just a few listens. (That particular talent also gets an airing when they say back to you things you said months before. You'll rarely win an argument based on 'But I never said that!') If there's music playing in the background during your first date, and you end up being in a relationship, be prepared to be tested on what it was months down the line. Your heart will probably sink every time they look at you all gooey-eyed when a song comes on the radio, and say, 'Aah, do you remember where we were when this was playing?' Make the wrong guess and you'll get a long lecture from a place called Hurt.

The whole issue of sound is complex. Loud voices can distract and annoy Nightingales, noisy nightclubs in which it's too loud to talk seem pointless, but empty restaurants where it feels like everything you say is being overheard can feel intimidating. The right sound level creates the right ambience, but each 'right' is going to be unique to the moment.

Après first date

If the first date goes well, Nightingales will probably call you before you get home, just to tell you they had a good time. Remember I said if you go out with a Sound bird to make sure you have the best mobile deal available? As the relationship develops, they are going to want to talk to you several times per day, and they will get a huge kick if you call them 'just to hear their voice'. Sound birds know you care because you tell them, which is a lot simpler than Sight birds, but that simplicity comes with a health warning; when you get to the point in your relationship where you are happy to say, 'I love you', you have to mean it.

Nightingales are tremendously sensitive to tone, so if you say it flippantly, or while you have trapped wind, not only won't they believe you, it will hurt their feelings. After a few dates they will have a repertoire of the tones you use to express a range of emotions lodged in their brain. There's a simple rule at work here: if the words don't match the tone you use to say them, the tone is believed. They have a moment when you said 'I love you' (which they believed) stored in their heads like an mp3 file, and that's what it's compared with. Fail the sincerity-matching test and you'll be in big trouble. And, a final bit of advice in this area, compliment them often. Anything good you think about them on the inside, share with them on the outside – your loving words are gifts.

Nightingales don't tend to welcome silence. Their houses will always either have music playing, or the television on 'for company'. Outside of the house earphones will be a semi-permanent fixture in their ears, even during the run-up to something else, like an evening at the theatre. Silence is a thing to be filled, so a career as a librarian would be a torture. Cosy evenings in watching the TV will involve long periods of live-pause as they interrupt the programme with some prompted recollection, discussion of a plot twist, or something that happened at work today that simply has to be told right now. This can be vexing I know, but do your best to be patient, and be careful with your criticism. The 'sticks and stones' adage doesn't apply here; words do hurt them, and it's unlikely they'll ever forget something painful you say that wounds them.

As sky birds, Nightingales are going to avoid detail like

it's infectious, so they'll be happy to leave organising things to you quite early in the relationship. They also get bored very quickly with anything they consider menial or just plain tedious, and that's a lot of everyday things, so tidiness doesn't tend to be high on their agenda, unless it's their CD collection. They'll talk for ages about anything they're interested in, and in detail, but are likely to have a low tolerance for *your* detail.

What excites them are patterns and possibilities. They have big ideas and get madly excited about them. Often they're like hurricanes, vast amounts of wind that's generated in a short space of time, which then just blows itself out. Just because they suddenly start talking about a new hobby, or moving house, or country, don't take it as read that they'll see it through; often it's just the fun of playing with the possibility, of staying up late and talking about it over a bottle of wine. You could be one of these new excitements, and it can be intoxicating to be caught up in this force of nature, as their feelings for you buffet you in a storm of words. It's a storm that might last a lifetime, or blow out overnight. It's the same with all sky birds. Joining them in their passions is probably your best bet for keeping their passion for you alive.

Nightingales don't seem to be great respecters of rules, because they often don't notice them. They're much more 'let's see how this works out' kind of people and it often means they repeat the same mistakes, and can appear quite chaotic in the way they live life. They trust their instincts over evidence, and goals are often quite loose and vague. And they won't pack for a holiday until the morning of their flight.

Nightingales in a nutshell

- Talk a lot because they think on the outside
- Get bored easily by anything that is menial or detailed
- Music will be important to them
- Very sensitive to verbal criticism or praise
- Like to explore ideas and enjoy talking about possibilities
- Begin more things than they'll finish
- Make decisions based on their instincts more than hard evidence
- They know they're loved by being told, but the voice tone needs to be right

How to click if we're similar

- Be aware that neither of you is great at organising or keeping things in order. Help each other
- Have fun with the new things you take up, and remember you're both likely to pick up and drop interests regularly
- Music is likely to be important to both of you. If you share tastes, make it a big part of your life; if majorly different, talk about it. Don't push your partner's music out of their life
- Remember to give time to each other to talk, and that you listening is an important part of it for them, just as them listening is for you

How to click if we're different

- They need to talk in order to think, so give them ample chance to do so. A regular date where you just 'catch up' will be highly valued

- They'll enjoy talking about ideas that may not be practical or have any chance of actually happening Enjoy that with them, don't shut it down
- If you're a ground bird it's best if you do the organising, or subtly check if they are. They get bored with details and miss things
- Remember to say anything good about them that comes to your mind; they need to hear it to know you love them
- Bear in mind how sensitive they are to criticism. They won't forget anything you say to them

Let's talk about sex, baby

When it comes to making love, there is one main requirement that transcends physical attractors. You can be a hunk-muffin like Brad Pitt, or a sex siren like my wife (I hope you men are taking notes. It takes years to get this smooth), but if you're silent in the bedroom, the relationship is doomed. Nightingales like their partners loud. They're likely to talk during sex. It could be words of encouragement – hopefully not 'you're doing so much better than last time', but words that tell you they like what you're doing – or it could be talking dirty to you – you little mucky pup you – or talking you through a fantasy. They'll like to hear from you what they're doing well and what you'd like more of. If they're good lovers they'll be listening to your breathing and adjusting their timing and tempo accordingly. If they're bad lovers they'll be listening to their iPod. Ooh, music. It's a good idea, have some mood music playing in the background; just make sure you both agree about what it is. A Eurovision compilation doesn't work for everyone.

Their favourite positions are likely to be ones where they can whisper in your ear. Kissing might not be a big deal because it cuts down on the sound, unless they're a ventriloquist, in which case you're probably in for one of the biggest shocks of your life during your first night together.

Phone sex can be a fun thing for them; they'll love to hear what you're wearing, but they'll enjoy hearing you orgasm more than anything. Just don't let them use it as a ring tone. You're bound to call when they're with their mother. Or yours.

Robins

When you listen to a robin sing it's easy to imagine that they're as caught up in the joy of their song as we can be as listeners. For their human equivalent, it can appear much the same: they can seem to like the sound of their own voices, but it's really only a part of their way of thinking. And they really do love all things audio. Record stores still selling vinyl records survive because of them – they'll regale you for hours about how much richer the sound is than CDs – and while they'll bemoan the poor-quality sound of an iPod in comparison, they'll probably own several because, like the lady who rode to Banbury Cross, they like to have music wherever they go. And bells on your toes is so 18th century.

Looking for love: how to click with a Robin

A variety of ways of meeting potential partners work for Robins, and often it will be influenced more by whether they are an extrovert or an introvert than by their Lovebird type. But what will be common, whether you meet them online, or at a concert, or at work, is how quickly vocal contact becomes important. They won't be anywhere near as keen on getting to know about you by email as on the phone, or face to face.

A meal is ideal for your first date, but not at a restaurant that rushes you through, and you'll probably need to go on somewhere else afterwards if the date is going well. Your Robin will have lots to tell you, and will want to know about you too, but often they'll dominate the first date, simply because they can be so intent on giving a good impression that they go off like a firecracker. If they muck up the first date by talking too much, leaving you feeling like they weren't interested in you, give them a second chance. As they calm down, more of a balance will emerge – but the balance will never be equal unless you're a Sound bird too.

Most Sound birds seem to need to hear what they're thinking on the outside of their heads to understand it, so they can seem to go on a bit (a lot), and often go in circles until they've sorted their heads out. Robins will also go into exhaustive detail about *everything*; there is no highlight reel with these guys. You will need to meet somewhere you can both be comfortable, and without distractions, because talking is going to be the main event.

Après first date

You can mistake the phone bills of Robins for their mortgages since, like Nightingales, they'll think nothing of ringing you four to ten times a day – often seemingly just to hear your voice. Remember, while this might be annoying sometimes, it's also a compliment. You have a voice that makes them feel good. That's pretty cool, isn't it? Sight birds will have photos and videos of their partners on their phone, Sound birds might have their partner's voice as their ring tone – I have my wife saying 'Hello Baby' in a mock Jerry-Lee Lewis style as my tone. I find it very cute, but it gets funny looks on the train.

Another thing you might notice about Robins is their habit of communicating fulsomely with everyone around them. At a restaurant they'll talk to all the waiters, at the checkout at the supermarket they'll start chatting to the lady behind them about something in her basket. If you visit places regularly together, it won't be long before everyone will know your Robin (especially if they are an extrovert) and either call a welcome as you enter, or dive into a cupboard.

Music is likely to be a big part of their scene. Huge. Often a Robin is able to create a playlist of their life, with each major event, both positive and negative, connected to a song. It's why they can be moved by a seemingly naff piece of music, while being the musical-taste police to everyone else. If Jedward was playing in the background when they received their disastrous exam results, they'll cry every time they hear them. Just not for everyone else's reasons.

For those Robins who need to speak their thoughts aloud, other people are a necessary accessory. You might find your Robin involving you in the smallest of decisions – like what to order for their meal. It's not actually indecision, and they may not take the advice you're giving; it's more a platform for them to do on the outside what most of us do on the inside: sort our thoughts out. This can be confusing, especially if they say: 'Can I ask you something?' and then talk at you for ten minutes without giving you any room to speak. But remember, they don't mean to be rude. They are using you as a sounding board and they are interested in your input. You can always gently interject.

Silence is a challenge for Robins. Sometimes it will be an absolute requirement; if they're deeply involved in something, any noise can be immensely distracting, but for the most part they'll struggle with it. At home there's likely to be a sound-creating machine in every room, whether it's a TV, a radio, or a sound system, and any room in use will have it switched on. As you can imagine, they see meditation as a form of torture.

From your first meeting, they'll be learning your voice. In no time at all they'll be able to identify your mood from the subtlest of cues in your intonation. They'll know when you say yes, but mean no; they'll know when you say 'fine' that everything really isn't. They'll be able to pick up in the subtlest hesitations your unease, and even spot the things left unsaid amidst the things that were. This can mean that you'll feel nurtured and understood – it's very hard to hide something from a Sound bird unless you stay mute. It also means that you need to take care with how you say things.

Words can wound them more than anything else (except something that actually wounds them). If you say something you don't mean, or that is unkind, they'll never forget it – or let you forget it. So even if you'd let it go and move on, they won't. Just remember, words are weapons.

Robins have an amazing ability to recall conversations verbatim. You'll soon learn this, because they might regurgitate whole meetings with colleagues, often accompanied by accents and mannerisms – Sound birds are often excellent mimics. On the plus side, when you're being affectionate, be aware that words are like their currency of love. Telling them how you feel about them will be a regular requirement, and if you ever throw a casual 'love you' at the end of a call, they may think something's wrong, because the way you said it didn't match the way they have it recorded in their heads when you did mean it. I've also found that saying it second after them doesn't count either. Say how you feel, say what you appreciate about them, tell them how great their butt looks in those trousers whenever you notice it. Don't waste a thought by keeping it to yourself, it's all money in the love account.

Robins like to know where they stand. They make decisions based on hard evidence, not their gut feelings (or anyone else's), and the more evidence there is, the happier they'll be. When you get to the point in your relationship where you decide to have a nice weekend away, don't think it's going to be a five-minute search on Trip Advisor. There will probably be brochures, or days of being sent weblinks to possible locations, and a D-Day-like briefing session where you work through the possibilities and plan a schedule.

Nothing will be left to chance, and the first half an hour of the car journey will probably be spent going through the checklist you went through before you left. Spontaneity probably won't appear on the checklist; Robins rarely pack any.

This liking for information extends to you. Robins will want to be kept in the loop about your life, in detail. When they ask you, 'How was your day?' (usually after they've told you about theirs) they won't be satisfied with 'It was good.' They might even consider that evasive or that you are being secretive. What made it good? Was it all good? What was wrong with the bits that weren't? Who said what to whom? How's Nancy after the operation? When you introduce your new partner to your friends or colleagues, you might be surprised how they seem to know them already. It's because your Robin will have been absorbing everything you've said about them since you met, filing it away in the Rolodex that is their head.

Being ground birds, Robins have rules. They can be very particular about the way things should be done, and often mistake their way for the only way. As you get to know them you are bound to transgress these rules, sometimes because they're just so peculiar to them, and sometimes because you just can't care. That's as it should be; you need to push against your Robin every now and again, or else you'll find yourself standing in the kitchen wondering what you've forgotten to do that's really, really important . . . to them. You will be instructed, and lectured, and they'll get exasperated at your failure to do things that are just so obviously necessary to the good order and preservation of society, but sometimes it will do them good to find that rules not adhered to don't actually cause the Earth to stop spinning on its axis. And, no, that wasn't a passive-aggressive sentence aimed at my wife. Yes it was.

Robins in a nutshell
- Talk a lot because they think on the outside – tend to use others as a sounding board
- Like to know the detail of everything – and tend to think that everybody else does too
- Make decisions based on facts rather than intuition
- Music likely to be very important to them
- Have rules, and take personally people not following them
- Like to plan rather than be spontaneous
- Very sensitive to criticism and will remember unkind words forever
- They know they're loved because you tell them, in a voice tone they've stored under 'sincere'. And following their rules will get you points too

How to click if we're similar
- Get to know each other's rules. If any conflict, talk them out, otherwise you can end up being passively aggressive
- If music is a shared passion make it central to the time you spend together. If your tastes are different make sure you honour theirs, not try to get them to change
- Schedule regular 'catch-up' time together so you can talk at length. And remember to listen as well as speak Sharing is caring

- You're both most comfortable when things are organised, and decisions have been exhaustively researched. But sometimes just flip a coin, it'll be good for both of you

How to click if we're different

- Robins need to talk – probably more than you do. They need to hear about your day in detail, and tell you all about theirs. Be patient
- Do your best to honour their rules, they're important to them. If some of them drive you mad make sure you bring this up and talk about it
- Create situations where music is part of a good time you're having together. Make a note of what you've both enjoyed and play it when you're together – it'll become a positive anchor for your relationship
- Unless you're a ground bird too, it's probably best, and easiest, if they do the organising. They enjoy it, they're good at it, and they'll nag you less about whether you've done what was needed, and in the right way (their way)

Let's talk about sex, baby

In the bedroom you can probably guess what you need. Sound proofing. If you tend to enjoy sex quietly, then there is a danger that you're not the partner for a Robin. I've heard that in some countries, belching after a meal is a sign of appreciation. Well, with a Robin, screaming is the sexual equivalent – not faking it, obviously, and they'd probably be able to tell anyway (unless you've had to fake it every time). They'll be listening to the sounds you make and the rate of your breathing as a means of gauging how successful they're being at giving you pleasure. They're probably not even aware of it, but they'll be aware of your silence, and it's likely to kill the mood. Often they like to talk dirty to you, or you to them, and so they often favour positions where they can whisper into your ear, or have their ear whispered into. Their name used during sex, instead of God's, will go down well too.

Music can be something that sets the mood, so having some music that works for both of you can be something that builds over time into a useful anchor – after a while, playing favourite tunes from your sex playlist, in the background over dinner, can be a nice flirtatious precursor to the main event. Of course if Tesco play one of your tunes while you're shopping you might have to switch to Waitrose afterwards.

Doves

The one thing Doves can't stand is discomfort. They are not the type to cram their feet into uncomfortable shoes in the hope of making an impression. Their dress style can range from whimsically eclectic, to fashion train wreck, but there's one thing that'll be common: nothing will be scratchy, or pinch, or make them too cold or too hot.

Looking for love: how to click with a Dove

In a modern world, Doves can feel a bit left behind, because often they're not fans of technology; many actually believe that computers have a vendetta against them. For that reason, online dating may not be for them – and also they really need to be with someone to know if they're going to be attracted to them. Doves and Swans are the types who can feel a jolt of electricity when they see someone they like, and they'll often act impulsively on that.

Feeling birds are very much about energy and so are directly affected by whether they are introverts or extroverts. If they're introverts, then they'll probably be quite passive and rely a little too much on life bringing their soul mate to their door, so they need to help things along a little by agreeing to be dragged to events by their friends, rather than just trust to the laws of attraction – even the universe needs a little help now and then. Extroverts will have an easier time because they're likely to have plenty of interests through which they'll meet people, and no inhibitions about approaching them – these are your archetypal flirts.

Après first date

It tends to be hard not to like Doves because they're usually very good at making people around them feel good. One of the key ways they do this is by taking care of others. They'll be the first to spot someone struggling with their shopping and offer help; they'll be the first to drop everything and go to a friend in need. They are easily hurt by unkindness, towards themselves, or others, and may even have stopped watching the news or reading newspapers because of how strongly they react to suffering. From the beginning you're likely to be wrapped in a warm fuzzy blanket of caring. If you're the independent type who takes longer to get close to people, you might find this a bit suffocating, but remember that the intention is good.

Many Feeling birds talk quite slowly. At the extreme of their type they're the kind of person whose sentences you want to finish, or at least find where to change their batteries. It doesn't mean they're slow or stupid – although they often leave school believing that – it's just that words are a long way from feelings, so they can take a while to find the right ones. Once they've warmed up to their subject they're generally fine, so on an early date just give them time to get comfortable with what they're trying to say. Don't pressure Doves to go any faster at anything than they already are – Sight birds often scare them with their high-speed responses, and a Sound bird's wall of words can make their heads vibrate, so pacing is particularly important.

Connecting with Doves is a lot about touch. They can sometimes seem flirtatious or forward because, from quite soon after meeting someone, they can be touching them as part of their way of communicating. They live in a world where people seem to get the wrong idea about them, because they're just being friendly, so don't get too excited when they start stroking your arm over dessert; they'll probably do that to the waiter when they pay the bill.

Think of it more as punctuation than invitation – you'll know when the touch turns to things more primal. And if you upset them, you'll know that too. They'll withdraw into their shells like a tortoise, and give you the full force of a cold shoulder. They can't think of anything worse, so you'd better notice.

Sex is often seen as an obvious expression of love, and

even support and comfort, so if you've had a bad day don't be surprised if they try to make your day better that way. Male Doves, in particular, tend to think that sex solves everything and can be a bit miffed when their attempts at ironing the kinks out of their partner's day are rebuffed. Dove women, on the other hand, will tend to withhold sex if they're not feeling close to you because it doesn't 'feel' right, so checking the wind direction of a female partner's mood is a good idea.

Doves and Swans seem to run on rechargeable batteries. When it gets near their bedtime, it doesn't matter how much they're enjoying your company, the light in their eyes will start to flicker as they start shutting down – so don't start watching a film anywhere near bedtime. Don't take it personally. On a similar note, many Doves aren't that hot first thing; the duvet seems to hide their 'on' switch. It can seem like an act of cruelty to tip them out of bed in the morning, so when it gets to that moment when you wake up together, do it gently, or risk that cold shoulder I mentioned being aimed your way for the rest of the day.

Doves live very much in the present, so they often don't really think ahead or see consequences very clearly. It can make them great fun and spontaneous, but it can also mean that if they have a bad day it can really bog them down in a negative mood. Rather than being able to look ahead like the rest of us, and see the day as just a moment in time, they tend to react as if it's the way things are always going to be.

In the early days of dating it can also mean that they are a bit up and down emotionally, seeming to run hot and cold: one moment really into you, other times, not so much. Often this will just be a product of the day they've had prior to meeting up with you, and the mood might take a while to shift. Bear in mind that if Doves arrive on a date in a bad mood, they may not be able to distinguish between being in a bad mood because of work and being in a bad mood with you. If that's the case, then pacing is important. Absorb their mood as best you can, gently talk them round and encourage them towards doing something they enjoy. Acts of service are a big indicator of love for them, so look for things that will please them, and that they'll find caring. Hopefully that will lift their mood, and if it doesn't, at least it may shift it away from you.

This tendency to live in the present can have an impact on long-term plans, which are not a Dove's forte. Just because they've agreed to something six months away doesn't mean they'll still agree when you get closer to it; they may not even feel they were ever really bound in the first place. Doves are also not a fan of delaying gratification; they'd rather have the one chocolate now than three chocolates tomorrow. Because tomorrow they'll say they didn't mean it, and still expect three.

When it comes to where they put their attention, most Feeling birds are balanced, but some will tend to have their 'feeling radar' either focused on other people, or on themselves. The distinction between 'self' and 'others' is particularly relevant to Feeling birds. For 'self'-focused Doves, how they feel is the first order of the day. This can make them seem selfish or self-centred, and certainly high maintenance, but many of them really are highly sensitive to the world around them. They notice sunlight being too strong, noises being too loud, clothes labels being scratchy, and the mattress being too hard or too soft. They seem to be searching for the Goldilocks moment in everything, never quite finding it, at least not for long.

This tends to give them an incredible connection to their body, which, on the plus side, gives them an enjoyment of comfort we can only imagine, and heights of sensual pleasure that require broad-minded neighbours.

Doves who are more 'others'-centred can be incredibly attuned to the emotional temperature around them, and seem to 'live' other people's feelings. They'll pick up an atmosphere between people as soon as they walk in the room; they'll know someone's had a bad day by the way they put the key in the door – it's very hard to keep a worry or a surprise from them. They can also elect themselves responsible for the world running smoothly, at least their world. Their friends, family and their date will be monitored for their wellbeing, and they'll sacrifice themselves to make sure everything is fine with everyone – this can often be at the expense of their own needs. They also have a tendency to bottle up their feelings until the pressure gets too much. 'Others' Doves don't lose their tempers often, but when they do, stand well back. The good thing is that it tends to blow over quite quickly; all Doves tend to be good at not bearing grudges.

Extrovert, 'others' Doves are really party people and get a high from good atmospheres, just as they can be crushed by bad ones. More than anyone, these are the ones who seem flirty because they offer hugs and cuddles to all and sundry at the drop of a tear. In a very real sense, they communicate through their skin. If they're deprived of physical contact they can quickly suffer, and they often have a pet to fill any stroke-gaps in their day. With physical touch being so natural to them, it may come as a surprise to find that they might be a bit jealous of the hugs their partners give others who might be construed as competition, possibly because they project their own feelings on to this other person. So be careful.

As sky birds, Doves will hate anything that requires repetition of a task they consider menial (what they mean is boring), so if you ever combine bank accounts, guess who'll be doing the balancing of the books? They're at their best providing the big ideas, not attending to the details.

They're likely to be creative, particularly with arts, and quickly pick up new physical skills – show them a dance move and they'll probably mimic it in a few moments. Hobbies will nearly always involve their hands more than their heads. They're practical, and likely to be able to build a house from scratch, strip an engine, bake like an angel, beat you at any sport you mention, and avoid anything written. Academia is rarely a comfortable place for them. Often these guys accumulate a host of skills over time, because they're butterflies, flitting from one interest to another. They don't have attention deficit, they're always paying attention to something; it's just that lots of things can get them excited. And why not? You are going to be glad of their skill set somewhere down the road: they are very practical people.

I joked earlier about Feeling birds being poor navigators, and I find this is true if they score low in the quiz as Sight birds, they just don't visualise very well – so be ready for them to get lost finding their way to you on a first date. Best to let them pick where to meet. Another cute thing you may notice is how they'll confidently leave a shop and stride down the street, before realising they're walking in entirely the wrong direction for where they want to go next.

Doves in a nutshell
- Much prefer face-to-face contact to the use of any technology
- Very sensitive to the moods of others
- Comfort is very important to them
- Live in the moment and don't tend to plan ahead
- Are practical rather than academic
- Make decisions based on their feelings and intuition
- Get bored easily with the mundane
- Slow starters at most things, but warm up
- They know they're loved through touch and the things that are done for them to make their life nicer

How to click if we're similar
- Neither of you is great at planning or organising, so help each other
- Make sure you create plenty of time for physical connection – not just sex, but hugs on the sofa
- Remember that having someone do something for you feels as good for your partner as it does for you, so strike a balance
- Be aware that mood strongly affects the both of you, so work at creating good ones

How to click if we're different

- Pace them. They may not be fast out of the gate, but they do warm up. Give them time and don't make them feel bad for taking longer than you to think through things
- Make sure you create opportunities for touch. Even just the act of holding hands in public can be highly significant to them
- Because they're so connected to their emotions, they can be a bit up and down. Learn to ride the wave

Let's talk about sex, baby

When you get to the stage in your relationship when hugging moves to the next level, remember that sensation is everything. Often Doves prefer the light out, just so they can feel you better. There'll be times when a quickie will be right, but more often they like a bit more of a sensual build-up. If you can massage you're on to a winner. If you can't, I recommend you learn; it will pay you dividends. If they're a 'self' Dove, then they'll keep you busy meeting their needs, which is more fun than I just made it sound. If they're an 'others' Dove, then it's likely that you are going to get to know the feeling of last night's baby oil sticking to your clothes pretty well. All positions work for them, and if they have their hands free, so much the better. Unless you've tied them. Consensually. With something that doesn't chafe, obviously.

All things to do with sensation are possible with Feeling birds, so introducing smells and tastes into the bedroom can be a turn-on – but avoid anything that leaves crumbs or has pips. So that thing you do with a bourbon biscuit is off the menu.

Swans

This is a bird noted for its serenity and poise, until something disturbs its peace. It's not so different with Swan people. They are very sensitive, both in terms of their emotions, and their physical sensitivities. If you arrive at your first date with them on anything other than a perfect day, weather-wise, they'll almost certainly have a range of clothing options in case it gets too hot, or becomes a bit chilly later on. If they've had a bad day, it might take them a while to shake that off, which could make the start of the date a bit tricky. They're very 'in the moment' people, so their moods tend to be affected by whatever happens to be around them at the time.

Looking for love: how to click with a Swan

Swans might be a bit more methodical than their Dove cousins in their search for love, but not by much. They are unlikely to be comfortable with online dating and will much prefer opportunities that throw people together – fate is relied upon to help out rather a lot, and they're all expecting a Hollywood moment of accidental, and unlikely, coming together to eventually solve their problem. If they're introverts then their efforts might be limited to changing supermarkets regularly to increase the chance of random trolley bumpage, whereas extroverts will be happy trawling pubs and clubs for any hobbies they have. An extrovert Feeling bird is the classic flirt, highly tactile, and often extremely alluring in their physicality. Introvert Swans tend to depend more on the moody and mysterious vibe to bring people to them.

Après first date

Until you get used to their ways, you might find a Swan partner a little high maintenance. Actually, you still will even after you've got used to them. With their physical sensitivity, they have an instinctive grasp for where a draught will come from, and can spot a lumpy sofa from the other side of the room. Often life for them seems like a search for perfection – the best mattress, the most fragrant cup of coffee, the comfiest shoes. But, just when you think they've reached the pinnacle and they express satisfaction, you realise there's always going to be another peak to search for and climb. It's just their nature. It means that they often give waiters a hard time, because who doesn't warm a plate before putting food on it, or heat the milk for an Americano? Are they savages?

It's likely that you will quickly take to them, despite this aspect of high maintenance or perfectionism, because they tend to be kind, and warm, and caring. People feel better for being in their presence because so often it's like being wrapped in cosiness. They often make their way into the caring professions, but need to be careful because they can put the needs of others above their own and suffer from emotional burnout.

When you first engage a Swan in conversation it can be a bit of a slow starter. They're not always the most natural of conversationalists, and words are not their greatest strength. They may take a while to work out their thoughts in a sentence, and so can start one several times, or stop halfway and start a different sentence. Be patient, they've probably had a lifetime of people telling them to speak up or hurry up. If you're someone who speaks quickly, do your best to slow down and pace your speed to theirs, or it can overwhelm them and they'll probably shut down. There may be occasions when you want to find out where to put the key to wind them up, but patience is the only solution here, and they'll love you for it.

The education system doesn't really suit Feeling birds, and many leave school with a lack of belief in their intelligence, so are easily undermined. In truth, they're as intelligent as any other Lovebird, it's just that their intelligence manifests in the practical. They pick up things they're shown very quickly, and make great chefs, and electricians, and nurses and hardware engineers. Their interests are likely to involve using their body, whether it's yoga, or a sport, or an art.

With Swans, actions definitely speak louder than words, so it doesn't matter how smooth you are, or how great your compliments; it's what they see you doing to express that you care that will matter most, because that's what they'll be doing. I have a dear relative who was raised in a home where love was never expressed verbally, so to show her love she bakes you a cake instead. And, let me tell you, a cake baked with 'I love you' as an ingredient tastes like no other. That's quite a covert example, but in the main you'll be aware of how much effort Swans put into making your life nice. You'll be aware of it because if you don't notice and show appreciation you'll soon see how they can use their displeasure to turn the air around you frigid. And you can't blame them; if you show someone you love them by saying so, imagine if you've said it and that person just carries on as if they haven't heard? Well, that's how Swans feel if you don't pass comment on how much you appreciated them getting off the sofa and making you a coffee.

They also express emotion through touch. Hugs, cuddles and strokes are all part of their language of love – which can be confusing because they also offer them to people they've only just met as a normal part of their communication. This means that they can seem quite flirty, and will, no doubt, have wide-eyed stories to tell of how people have completely got the wrong end of the stick regarding their 'friendliness'.

As a couple, holding hands while out walking is a given. You know those old couples who walk down the road with a tandem Zimmer frame so they can still hold hands? One of them at least will be a Feeling bird. Sleeping with Swans can be like wearing a rucksack to bed, because spooning isn't optional.

Sex is a common expression of love, especially for male Swans, who can get criticised for thinking that sex solves everything. For them, it's just a natural way of expressing closeness, and all the things they feel that they don't have words for. For females, closeness tends to need to exist first. I don't talk much about gender generalisations, but this one is common enough to be worth the risk, because it can lead to lots of misunderstandings in new relationships. If you're the type for whom sex is the last thing on your mind after the day you've had with your boss, and your partner gets smoochie as a solution to it, this is so going to hit the wrong note. It's not that they don't understand you – they get that you're upset – they just misunderstand the solution. Just as you offering them a night at the cinema as a solution to their bad day isn't going to cut it for them.

For Feeling birds, sex is likely to be even more of a measure of the strength of the relationship than it is for other Lovebirds, whichever gender, because it's such an avenue for feelings to be explored and expressed. If it happens less frequently for some reason, like pressure at work, it can sometimes be mistaken for something being wrong, so it's important to talk about it – and maybe even schedule it in.

Which brings us to the way Swans like things. Like all ground birds, their way is the best way, and they can never quite understand why the world doesn't follow their rules. They often take it upon themselves to be the teacher, so from quite early in the relationship you might find yourself the recipient of some helpful ideas and suggestions about how much better it is to do a great range of things a certain way. I've been with my lovely Swan wife for about 15 years, and she's still discovering things I'm doing wrongly. I have yet to hang washing to her satisfaction. Only the other day I was shown how I was overlapping the towels too much at the top for optimum drying. For me, hanging a shirt by the sleeves is a quiet act of rebellion. You'll notice that Swans will like many things a certain way; rarely will they dare to just 'take it as it comes', about anything. They tend to love certainty, and can delay making decisions because they feel they don't have enough information to be sure. If there are only a couple of tickets left for that concert you wanted to see, but they're a bit more than you wanted to pay, best you make the decision, because they'll be checking other sites first. You'll need to be aware that when they say they like the table laid a certain way, it's part of what stops civilisation sinking into the barbarian mire, so be ready for a strong look if you fail to fold the napkins properly.

So learning their rules will grease the wheels of the relationship – at least it will if you follow them – but you also have to be careful that they don't steadily erode your sense of identity. It can feel as if you're a bit of a project, that they're trying to upgrade you for your own good, which, if you're happy as you are, can become a bit of a drag. But always remember that they're doing it, not because they're control freaks, but because they think they're being helpful. To maintain your self-esteem in the face of this gentle assault, tap into how their efforts are making you feel. If you notice you're getting irritable or exasperated, then it needs to become one of the things you talk about. Having a code word that lets them know that they're doing it too much can be helpful. I use the word 'bossy' in a playful tone, just as a gentle reminder that I'm feeling the weight of my wife's project management a little too much.

Swans aren't the fastest out of the blocks in the morning. If at all possible it's best to avoid talking until after 10am. When you've been together a while, bring them their favoured first beverage of the day while they wrestle with their eyelids, it will bring you brownie points – but maybe not after the first date; that could be trespass. But if it isn't, I'm not judging either. Energy is an interesting aspect of Feeling birds. They're usually active people who enjoy all kinds of sports and physical activities, but they can need regular refuelling, and enjoy a nap in the middle of the day, or the middle of a meeting. Keeping them awake when the sleep fairy comes calling is a fool's errand, so don't take it personally if they tip into the dessert during an evening out. It's probably more that it's been a busy day than a comment on you. Probably.

Swans in a nutshell
- Live in the present
- Their physical comfort is a big deal
- Can be slow to think of what to say, but emotionally very intelligent
- Highly tactile
- Organised and good at working with details
- Practical, they pick up physical skills very quickly
- Sports, dancing and crafts likely to be an interest
- Have rules that are important to them. See their partner contravening them as a sign of not caring

- They know they're loved by the way they're touched and hugged, and by the things that are done for them to make their life nice

How to click if we're similar
- Rules are important to both of you. Work out which ones conflict, and negotiate about them
- Both of you are quite organised, but neither is that great at future planning. Help each other, or recruit a sky bird friend
- Remember that things you do for your partner feel as good as the things they do for you. Get a good balance of giving and receiving
- Physical sensation is important. Make time for touching, and the pursuit of whatever physical activities you both enjoy

How to click if we're different
- Don't mistake their pursuit of comfort for being 'precious'. They really do feel things more sensitively than most others. Support their pursuit of perfection as patiently as you can
- Look for what areas of their life mean the most to them, and find ways to make them better
- Pace them. They might not verbalise things as quickly as you, but they'll be worth listening to. Don't rush them
- Their rules are important. Learn them, and follow them as best you can. If you disagree with them, then make sure you say so don't just trample over or ignore them

Let's talk about sex, baby

When it's time to take the relationship to the next level, it's going to be all about the sensation for Swans. It might well be that you both get swept up in a tide of passion and need no guidance from me, but if it's more of a planned, or semi-planned progression to the 'big night', then taking your time would be a great idea. Dim, or no lighting, so they can focus on how their (and your) body feels, a gradual, teasing build-up, maybe a bit of oil (massage, not vegetable), and lots of foreplay. If they are the kind of Feeling bird who focuses most on others, then they will delight in giving you pleasure, and feel short-changed if you deny it to them, thinking that you're being selfish. Let them enjoy your enjoyment, their turn will come. If they're more self-oriented, you'll soon tell, and you can only hope that your turn will come, but it won't be until they do.

All positions work, unless they're uncomfortable ones, and they'll like their hands free. Pleasant textures, like silk, can be part of the fun, but I'd steer away from chain-mail (if you only knew the research I've had to put into this book). Yoghurt, chocolate toppings and that sort of culinary experimentation might even appeal. It's a question of taste. Boom boom.

Kingfisher

When you first meet a Kingfisher you will often be struck by how precise they are. It's unlikely they'll be late; punctuality is usually very important to them. They'll be very clear about most things, from their career path to where their favourite place to take you on honeymoon is going to be. Kingfishers have a plan for everything, in fact they can't really get out of bed in the morning without making one. Spontaneity can be lacking, unless it's in the plan, so mucking them around by changing the time or locations of dates will make them impatient quite quickly.

Looking for love: how to click with a Kingfisher
Kingfishers will often approach looking for love like it's a military campaign, with no step missed out, no stone left unturned. Online dating will suit them perfectly in terms of the searching. The finding might be more problematic because their emails tend to be short and to the point – not necessarily the most romantic beginning. They'll probably have a list of what they're looking for in a partner, so the first date can end up like a job interview. Whether they'll enjoy dinner dating or other social gatherings as a means of finding romance will largely depend on their second Lovebird type – remember, Thinking birds usually have an underlying preference for Sight, Sound or Feeling – but if they do, they'll need time to interrogate . . . I mean chat with . . . their companion, so speed dating may not suit.

You can probably tell that my suggestion is going to be to chill out a little if you are a Kingfisher. Don't come over as too intense, work hard to let things naturally evolve and trust that the answers to your checklist will emerge from your conversation. This applies to any other dating medium you try; do your best to be chattier, and less to the point.

Après first date

In many cases, Kingfishers will be as happy to connect via email or text, as speak on the phone. Sometimes it might even seem they prefer it to actually meeting. Okay, that's a slight exaggeration! Kingfishers will develop such a strong sense of you inside their heads that they may not appear to miss you in the same way as some other Lovebirds.

Their emails can seem a little curt; like they're writing to a business colleague, rather than a potential lover. Straightforward, factual and to the point, they don't go much for emotions or social pleasantries.

Hello,

Sex tonight?

Best,

Tony

This is the kind of standard, and an x after their name is a sign they're really keen. Many Kingfishers are quite blind to the emotions of others. If you share a problem with them they're more likely to try to solve it than sympathise with you about it. They tend to try to keep away from their own emotions as much as they can. They won't want to watch a movie that could make them cry, and they won't want to open up about their feelings. In the early days – the first twenty years or so – they can come across as a bit remote, and even robotic. It's almost as if they have a switch; one moment they're dazzling company, the next, they've gone somewhere inside themselves where you can't follow or penetrate.

When I say dazzling company, I mean it. They often have a great sense of humour, love wordplay and puns and tend to be very quick-witted. What you have to understand about them is that they always have a dialogue going on in their head, and often it is louder and more compelling to them than real life. I'm a Thinking bird and my wife habitually snaps her fingers before saying something important, so I don't have to pretend I heard what she said.

Kingfishers like detail. They won't make a decision until they're sure they're right, and that surety usually comes from a meticulous examination of all possible evidence. Even a menu is going to take a while, unless they've been planning all day what they were going to eat.

One of the abiding truths about Kingfishers is that things have to make sense to them. If they don't, they simply won't do what they're being asked to, and they're likely to be less than kind to the person making the request. A by-product is the preponderance of insomnia clients who come from the ranks of Thinking birds. They lie in bed trying to work something out, and, until they have, sleep will elude them.

They do have a knack for problem solving, and this often informs their career choices. In a relationship it can frequently mean that they see themselves as the captain in charge of the ship, and that they know best. You need to push against that from early on, otherwise there is a risk of being smothered, even though their intentions are good. They are rarely satisfied for long, and have an appetite for learning new things, so anyone dating a Kingfisher will need to be tolerant of their need to have other passions. You might have to be shared with toy trains or salsa dancing, but there are worse infidelities.

Kingfishers can be quite difficult to live with because they like things their way. They can be quite rigid in their rules, and will have lots of them, and there is a level of expectation that others need to change towards their way of doing things, right down to choices of food and music. Partners of Kingfishers really do have to be strong to maintain their own identity and if that doesn't sound much fun, go back to the bit about them being dazzling company. It's a balance.

As Kingfishers process things by going inside their heads, it's possible to lose their attention part-way through a conversation. By the time they come back to the real world they've lost track, but are probably scared to say so. It's why they'll often go on to do the very opposite of what has just been agreed. This tendency doesn't mean they're not interested in what is being said to them – in fact, the reverse is true. Think of it this way: you've said something so interesting that your Kingfisher has had to dive inside to think about it.

When you first start dating a Kingfisher you can be left wondering if they are actually into you. As I mentioned earlier, they may not feel the need to ring you much because they'll already have such a strong impression of you in their heads. Remember, Kingfishers don't tend to miss people like other Lovebirds. Often some of this reticence is about fear – they may have had experiences that cause them to fear being rejected, and their default position with matters of the heart is to deal with them from behind a barricade, which often results in the very rejection they fear. Persevere.

If they can learn to trust that you're with them for the long haul (I'm assuming here that you want to be) then they can really blossom, and feel less like they are observers of the world and more like participants. They may even watch a Reese Witherspoon film with you one day and get a bit misty-eyed.

This tendency towards emotional dissociation can extend to their bodies. Thinking birds can be amazingly disconnected from what their bodies are trying to tell them. They can be quite ill before they notice. They probably won't be aware that they're borderline hypothermic until someone throws them a jumper. Don't even bother to ask them where they got a particular bruise, because the chances of them knowing, or even being aware they have a bruise, are pretty remote. I ran a half marathon this morning before sitting down to write. Come lunchtime I was nearly welded in place in my chair. I'm waiting for my Feeling bird wife to return home, tut in utter disdain, and help me up. Thinking birds live in their heads. Their bodies are just a means of getting that head from one place to another.

When it comes to expressing their love, they may not. Out loud. If you say, 'I love you', the chances are they'll respond with 'Me too', but only in their heads, so they need encouragement to vocalise what they think in relation to their partners. That said, their second Lovebird preference will often provide clues, so familiarise yourself with the relevant entries too. For example, a Kingfisher with Swan as their second preference will go one of two ways. They'll either be much more comfortable with their feelings than others of their type, and more likely to seek physical contact as an expression of affection. They may even be a little more aware of sensation. Or, on the other hand, with feelings being closer to the surface they could be a bit Jekyll and Hyde-like, attracted to the emotions that rise so close, but scared of them at the same time, and so can be even more emotionally constipated than other Thinking birds. When drunk they might be far more open and effusive than they are when sober. It's a struggle between head and heart which is the biggest challenge in their lives to resolve.

If Robin is their second choice then they'll probably be much more talkative than a classic Kingfisher, and be more free with their compliments and general verbalisation of their feelings.

Kingfishers/Peacocks are probably the combination that best fit the description I've offered here. Quick, smart, and often separated from the world by a barrier of their own making.

Kingfishers in a nutshell

- Always have a plan, and like to stick with it. Can have a problem with surprises and spontaneity
- Spend a lot of time in their own heads; need time alone
- Can appear distant; don't tend to share their emotions
- Can feel they're on the outside looking in
- Their rules are very important to them, and they can be quite inflexible about them. Contravening them can be the same as not caring
- They make decisions based on evidence and hard facts
- Details matter; they don't like things that are imprecise or don't make sense

- They mainly know how they're loved according to their second Lovebird preference

How to click if we're similar

- You both like things a certain way – your way Negotiate about everything that matters to you
- Make time to actually share what you're thinking with each other
- Don't use each other to make shying away from emotions easier. Use your relationship to get more comfortable with them
- Both of you like to know the details of anything. This can slow your decision making. Sometimes flip a coin just to add some spontaneity

How to click if we're different

- Make sure they're listening to you before talking about anything important. Remember that not hearing what you said isn't a sign of not caring
- Their rules are very important to them. If any really bug you then make them part of an early conversation, otherwise do your best to honour them
- If you want them to agree to an idea, make sure you have the evidence for it ready. They don't trust gut instincts, especially other people's
- They struggle with emotions, both with expressing theirs and with being around other people's. They're not robots, they're just reluctant to let the barriers down. Encourage them gently

Let's talk about sex, baby

In the bedroom, again, their preferences are often taken from their second type, but there are some things I can generalise about. Firstly Kingfishers often see sex as a performance, as opposed to an opportunity for intimacy, and as such it becomes a thing to measure – especially in their own heads. They'll count orgasms and compare them against a chart in their head of previous times. There'll be the classic question, 'How was it for you?' – possibly even while holding a clipboard. The likelihood is that they'll be good at sex, because they'll have worked out how to be, but maybe not so good at making love.

I've also come across quite a few male Kingfishers who suffer from performance anxiety because of their internal voice. Throughout sex they will have a conversation going on in their head about how it's going, what they plan to do next, what they hope you'll do next (because often they won't ask). The problem can be doubt. Nothing causes a loss of erection faster than asking yourself the question, 'Is it still hard?' – so I've heard . . . Kingfishers' interior conversations can become a self-fulfilling prophecy. A way out of it that I've found works is to encourage them to tell you naughty stories. Give them a fantasy and leave them to spin a story, because they can only listen to one wavelength at a time – what they're saying out loud, or what they're saying in their heads.

Another thing is their liking for plans. It can kill the spontaneity. If you arrive at the door to the living room with your 'come hither' look on your face, and nothing else, and they've been planning to watch a particular programme on the TV all day, they'll struggle to change tracks. I remember one disgruntled wife saying how she'd surprised her husband one evening by leaving him to watch the TV while she went to dress in his favourite outfit – a basque with the full kit. Feeling very pleased with the result, she came back into the room and paraded in front of him. He was good enough to give her positive feedback, but got her to wait until the programme finished! And he probably thought she was being a bit inconsiderate. Now let me think . . . what was she coming to see me for . . . that's right, self-esteem issues and the stress of her divorce.

Owls

Of all the Lovebird types, these are the best in bed. I feel lucky to be one of them. Oh, and the funniest too. All the women I've slept with have agreed on that.

When you first meet an Owl date, you might have a challenge identifying them as an Owl because they'll be making an effort to stay outside their heads. It almost certainly won't last the evening, and at some point you might feel that you've lost their interest. Don't panic, or think this is about you. Sometimes they will just have to go inside and order their thoughts. Check where their eyes are looking for the biggest clue. They may come across as quite intense and passionate when you hit on something they're interested in, but it might be a slog if you stick at superficial small talk; they're not good at it, or at hiding their boredom when engaging in it.

Looking for love: how to click with an Owl
When searching for a date, Owls are likely to try most things – sometimes it will be whether they're an introvert or extrovert that will guide or limit their choices. On the whole, being able to peruse online and make quiet contact will suit most more than handling a speed or a dinner date scenario. They'll probably be quite content to get to know someone via email because it gives them time to sculpt a reply – they'll be quite particular with their words – and are often uncomfortable on the phone. If they can go from email to actually meeting they'll probably prefer it.

Après first date
The intensity of an Owl can mean that getting to know you feels more like an interrogation; not because it's in any way unfriendly or cold, just that they really like to look deep; they don't do shallow. This is not just about you; they'll tend to look deeply into everything, and hate it when they don't understand something or feel information is being kept from them. Good luck with keeping a secret. They're often excellent at spotting patterns and making intuitive leaps of understanding, so their guesses are always worth listening to; they'll often anticipate something about to happen before most other people.

Owls spend a lot of time in their heads. You'll have evenings with them when it feels like you're on your own because they're somewhere else. This is true, they are. Owls have a rich internal world they probably spend more time in than the real one. It's not uncommon for them to watch a whole TV programme and remember nothing of it because of some distracting internal dialogue. In many people's model of the world, talking to yourself is a sign of going mad; to an Owl it's the opposite – if they're in a situation where they have no time to 'go inside' they can get quite uncomfortable. Periods of silence will be an essential part of your relationship, which is why, if you're a Sound bird, this particular gig is going to be a tough one.

There will be times when you'll need to clap your hands or click your fingers to get an Owl's attention, so it's best not to start a conversation until you're sure they are with you; otherwise, halfway through, they'll either have to start bluffing or get you to start again, usually with an excuse to cover the fact that they weren't listening. It's not about being disinterested in you, or not wanting to be with you; it's just that they are easily pulled inside. Because of this, mayhem can reign around them and they'll have their head stuck in a book, totally oblivious to it all. I see it as a useful talent. My wife, not so much.

Owls often feel more like they're observers of life than actual participants. This can easily translate into them feeling that they don't fit in or belong, especially in new groups, and so meeting friends and family can be a bit of an ordeal for them; best not to rush it.

One of the signature features of an Owl is their relationship to their emotions. They may not be entirely divorced, but they're certainly estranged. My theory about Thinking birds is that experiences during their childhood may have led them to avoid their feelings. Or, in some cases, it's simply because they didn't get much of an opportunity to socialise. It's often through our interactions with other people that we become attuned to our emotional lives. For whatever reason, Owls are uncomfortable with emotions. They'll tend to avoid expressing them – so late nights talking about how you feel are definitely not high on their 'favourite ways to spend an evening' list – and they will tend to avoid situations where they might experience negative feelings themselves. For example, they probably just won't get the point of watching something that will upset them, so weepie films are out, but at least you're guaranteed a cup of tea when it gets to the bad bit in *Bambi*, because they'll leave the room to make it. They might even claim they got some dust in their eyes when they return.

If you're an emotional person, it's going to be a challenge for both of you. An Owl's first response to you being in distress is to do something that will relieve it, and that's usually by trying to solve or fix the thing that caused it. In a situation where you need to get to hospital, Owls are the perfect people for a crisis, but if what the situation needs is just for you to be heard, not a five-point plan on how to deal with your annoying work colleague, then they may seem a bit cold and pragmatic. Remember, it's just their way of trying to help, and it's something you can educate them about over time. In the same way, if an Owl actually shares a problem with you – and that will be quite rare, because they're devils for keeping their troubles to themselves until they've fixed them – then what they are likely to be after are some options and ideas, not an examination of how they feel, or even sympathy. For Owls, it's all about the solution.

Time is something you'll probably need to give if you

want this relationship to be all it could be. Owls can be great to be with; I've a number of ex-partners who'll attest to that; but they're not easy. Not because they try to be difficult, but because the way they maintain a distance from life can leave their partners feeling lonely and isolated. Also, the way they keep their emotions locked up means they can come across as robotic or uncaring, which can really inhibit the intimacy that grows out of a successful relationship, and it takes time to nurture their trust enough to give them the confidence to fully connect.

Often one of the feelings they're scared of is rejection, so the prospect of letting you get close to them both appeals and scares the bejabbers out of them. With time and patience your relationship could be the place where they learn to trust, engage with their feelings, and join the world more fully, and I think that's something worth working on if you have feelings for an Owl. But then I would.

When they're on the outside of their heads they can be great company. They tend to be witty and quick, good with words and wordplay. Their default position is 'interested', so they're great people to learn from and explore with. It's likely that they'll hop from one interest and passion to the next, and on each occasion demonstrate a laser-like focus that you'd swear means they've discovered their life's passion, only to abandon it when the next thing comes along. It means they'll have a range of knowledge – useful and other-wise – and will often be able to do things that surprise you. In order not to feel abandoned by an Owl, if you can genu-inely join them in their interests it would be a real plus. It really is just part of the deal with them; they have a very low tolerance for boredom and need things to feed their curiosity.

This avoidance of boredom is part and parcel of being a sky bird. Owls hate detail, so they'll usually do anything it takes to get themselves out of the mundane. They'll regularly forget to pay their credit cards if left to themselves, forget to make appointments or organise something that you'd both agreed was their job – or at least forget some part of the organising that turns out to be key, like checking the date the concert is actually on. I have a sky bird friend who has taken her family to several weddings of people she doesn't know, because she turns up on the wrong day. It must cost a fortune in extra presents.

Owls can seem secretive, not just because they spend so much time in their heads, but because when you ask them a question they'll tend to give you a minimal answer. If you ask them how their day was, 'okay', for them, is a perfectly reasonable answer. If you're not a sky bird you might just like a little more flesh on the bone, and if you're a *strong* ground bird you'd probably like a minute-by-minute account, so that's likely to be an ongoing dissonance you'll need to work on.

Owls in a nutshell
- Spend a lot of time in their heads
- Love to explore new ideas and dreams
- Better at starting things than finishing them
- Not very organised and get bored very quickly with anything they consider menial or repetitive
- Passionate about their interests, but don't talk trivia comfortably. Like to look deeply into things

- Need time alone to think
- Not emotionally expressive
- Good with words
- They know they're loved mainly by their second Lovebird preference

How to click if we're similar
- Find similar interests and passions
- Make sure you regularly spend time talking to each other about what's in your heads
- Work together to organise yourselves; don't leave it to just one of you
- Don't use your relationship to hide from your emotions. Use it to explore them

How to click if we're different
- Not hearing you doesn't mean they're not interested. Make sure you have their attention before you begin
- They're suspicious of emotions, so pace them; it'll take a while for them to open up or be comfortable with yours
- Things need to make sense to them or they'll dismiss them, so if you're looking to persuade them, work on your argument first
- They love new ideas and learning things. Incorporate that into dates you plan

Let's talk about sex, baby
When it comes to that moment in the relationship when things turn physical, it's likely that your Owl will have it

all planned out. They do love a plan. While they can be more spontaneous than their Kingfisher cousins, don't be surprised if what you think is a romantic moment, that just happens to turn into *the* moment, has been orchestrated in some way. As I said earlier, it's more difficult to generalise about Thinking birds, because their second preference will have a major impact on the things that turn them on, but there are a couple of pointers. As with Kingfishers, sex is often seen as a performance. Turning sex into lovemaking is probably going to be one of those things that arises from the time you give to your partner, but it should be a fun part of the process. Owls are usually good and very creative in bed – at some time it's probably been one of their major hobbies – so check the loft for old partners. With it being a performance, your enjoyment is likely to be a major deal for them, so be patient if they seem a bit too interested in how many times you came, whether it's the best sex you've ever had, what makes it better etc. It's both the competitive element of the performance, and their need to learn how to get better at anything they do. It's just that an interrogation isn't usually as welcome after sex as a simple cuddle.

Some Owls might suffer from performance anxiety, from this 'need to be good', and from their internal dialogue. Make no mistake, they are having a conversation with themselves about how the sex is going, while they're doing it, so if there is reason for doubt – maybe you're not responding, maybe they're not – then it can cause them problems. For example, for a man, asking yourself, 'Am I still erect?' is a sure-fire way to point things downhill.

Getting them to talk dirty to you, or verbalise their fantasies, is one effective way around this, as the external talk
cancels the internal.

Owls are likely to be quite experimental, so I hope you're
broad-minded. Bear in mind how they can have a whole
conversation with you in their head and mistake it for one
that you actually took part in. So if they suddenly appear
in the doorway with a feather boa, a trifle and a neighbour
dressed as a Ghostbuster, this might be one of those times.
They do need to learn to express their ideas out loud, *and*
hear your agreement.

CHAPTER SEVEN

How to put it all together

I know a lot about lonely. After one of several occasions when I was left for someone else, I wrote this poem, and called it, 'This must not be true'.

> *In this world we're all alone, of that be in no doubt,*
> *From the narrow squeeze into the world, to the box that*
> > *takes us out.*
> *Ignore the honeyed words of love that twine two hearts*
> > *as one,*
> *Another's touch is only that,*
> *Now there,*
> *Now going,*
> *Now gone.*

I know a lot about lonely, and I've learned a lot about being loved since. The main thing I'm convinced about is that you've got to be happy *being* you for someone to be happy being *with* you. I mentioned at the start of the book how many clients come to me with things that are making them unhappy, from eating disorders to addictions, anxiety disorder and depression, and that what I find underlying it, on most occasions, is a lack of liking for themselves. In fact, when I ask them a standard question of mine, 'On a scale of 0–10 how much do you like yourself' I rarely get higher than 2/10 as an answer from these categories of clients, and rarely more than 5/10 for ANY client, even if they only want to stop biting their nails or lose a few stone in weight.

That's why I began the book with some exercises and techniques dealing with your confidence, and let's not fool anyone, just doing them for a few weeks isn't going to transform you into a person with consistently high self-esteem in all areas of your life, but it can be a beginning, which can be turned into a habit; a habit of having fun being yourself. From wherever you begin to notice this happening, it can spread into every other area of your life too. My field is often labelled 'Personal Development'. But personal development isn't a place you can visit and leave with the job done; it's an ongoing, organic process that has to form part of your everyday life. We are all changing, it's inevitable, but what I observe is that most people change into more of what they've always been – the unhappy just grow unhappier. What I believe, to the marrow of my bones, is that we can take control of that change, and become more of who we'd like to be. It's not easy, but it's possible. And relationships can be a great place to practise, because they create some of the biggest challenges to our view of our 'self'. It's also a necessary place to practise, because until you like yourself, you're unlikely to risk showing the 'real' you to someone you're attracted to so the relationship is doomed from the start by your lack of authenticity.

As a result of reading this book, what I'd like you to begin to do is apply the lessons in it to the people you meet. Not just those you have a romantic eye on, but everyone. Begin to look for the differences I've labelled, and when you spot them, match them to that person's behaviour, look for how that difference is influencing the way they interact with the world, and begin to practise using that understanding of their behaviour to improve your communication with them. This comes with a health warning – watching people in this way can become addictive. Don't let people in on the secret; it's much easier if you do it covertly. Then, as you improve your observational powers, they will be more naturally available to you when you get into a dating situation, and, I promise you, it will make you feel more empowered when you meet people for the first time. A lucky by-product is that, if you get stuck in one of those boring dates that you know is a once-ever, you can figure out what it is that's making it boring. Believe me, it helps to pass the time. Of course, you might wonder if they're doing the same thing.

Finding the right person for you is largely a matter of numbers. As the Lottery advert used to say, *you've got to be in it to win it*. I've spoken to lots of single people who moan about never meeting anyone, and when I ask them about their lives it becomes obvious that their only hope of meeting the right one is if they're the Pizza delivery person. You've got to get out there in the world and bump into folk. I know that's going to be a challenge if you're an introvert, in which case deliberate targeting through online dating or meet-a-mate events is going to be less of a drain on your energy than trawling the local pubs and clubs every night. Which would obviously be extrovert heaven.

What I hope I've given you in this book is an idea of why some ways of meeting a potential mate might appeal to you, and some won't – not necessarily so you automatically avoid the less appealing, but just so you know why – after all, they're still sources of date material. By knowing the ways you're likely to find less comfortable, you can do something about it. Or just play to your strengths and use the ways you will like; it's your choice.

The key thing is that, when you're with someone for whom you feel a spark, or an inkling there might be a spark, or someone you just want to rub up and down against to see if that would cause a spark, be yourself. From the beginning, whether it's by email, text, chat in a bar, or waving flags from opposite hills, be yourself. I hate the phrase, 'be yourself, because everyone else is taken', because I didn't think of it first, but it's true, and anyway, putting on a front is counter-productive. If you pretend to be someone you're not, you're either faced with a lifetime of being someone else, or saving up for your partner to be disappointed in you later. The person who will love you for a lifetime needs to recognise you, so commit to working on your confidence, project a positive outcome on everything, and don't make everything about you, about whether you're lovable or not. Trust me, you are.

The tools I've given you, to create rapport by matching or mirroring your date's behaviour, to watch their eyes and listen to their words to identify their Lovebird type, and to use interest, thoughtfulness and kindness, are going to be brilliant for helping you focus on the quality of your communication, and by far the most important tool you have is your attitude. As Ashton Kutcher said in a speech at the Teen Awards in 2013 (I know!), 'The sexiest thing in the entire world is being really smart. And being thoughtful and being generous. Everything else is crap, I promise you.' I think he's right. Being nice will attract nice – I'm hoping that if you've got to the stage where you'd find this book appealing, you've moved past any attraction to 'bad' people. That's a sign that you're smart, as is buying this book . . . People who make you feel less good about yourself are wasting your life; dump them. The right person for you will help you believe in yourself; will help you be more than you ever thought you could be.

When I look back at my poem now, I still find the first part true. We are alone. But we're complete, we have everything we need within us for the journey through life, we don't need someone to substitute for something lacking in us – it's that mistake that drives our problem with being ourselves – we just want someone to share the fun and the challenges along the way. We're alone, but if we like ourselves, we can share who we are with another, fully and completely. We can reveal our heart, and trust what intimacy can bring, and maybe, if we're lucky, another's touch will be with you for as long as breath remains.

So, go and find some frogs to kiss, and be kind to them

if they don't turn out to be your Prince or Princess, because they will be someone else's, and you don't want to damage them. Some days it'll be your turn to be the frog, but there will come a time when your lips meet, and you'll know. That's when the hard work starts. I hope this book will help you with that too, and as your relationship lengthens and deepens, *Lovebirds* can help you further.

Good luck.

Acknowledgements

Unusually, most of the people who deserve my gratitude I don't actually know. As a compulsive observer of people, I've listened to conversations in every possible location over many years, and probably learned something about people from every one. I have a theory that people tell you about themselves whatever they're talking about, and in this book I've taken that belief and used it to help you find the person who has so far eluded you. If I'm successful, you'll also owe a debt to these unknown collaborators. Who knows, you may have been one of them. Come to mention it, you do look familiar.

There's also a sizeable army of friends, colleagues and clients – especially those clients who sought my help with relationship issues – who've also been an invaluable resource, both with their stories and their insights. I've been blessed by the people I've met in my life who fall into any one of these three categories, and I only wish there was space to name you all.

When it comes to individually thanking people, the first who gets a mention is my wife Rebecca, because this book was her idea – as I felt compelled to remind her when I found myself stuck in a hot room, writing, on a sunny day.

In a meeting with my publishers, when we were discussing possible follow-ups to *Lovebirds*, it was she who saw the obviousness of a prequel. I just hope I've done a better job than the *Star Wars* writers managed.

Then my publisher, Mark Booth, needs to make an appearance. He was the person to first have faith in me within the publishing world and has maintained it ever since, along with a knack for good advice, and commendable patience. Thank you.

And finally, my editor Sarah Westcott. We hadn't worked together until this book, but I really hope we can again. She took such care in making this a better book, and putting up with my sulks and pouts when she made good suggestions I didn't happen to like – although I still think the Tracey Emin joke was funny! My sincere thanks to her for her skill, her diligence and her ground bird exactitude.

In no way do my two miniature Schnauzers, Fred and Betty, deserve any kind of thanks, just because some of my best ideas sprang from my walks with them. I doubt that the joy they bring us was any help at all either, so they can just forget any chance of being mentioned here. Don't look at me like that with those eyes you two . . . no . . .